THE HALF OF iT

CMUP Drama
Wendy Arons, Series Editor

Other works by Domenick Scudera

Full-Length

Gilgamesh: An Epic of Heroes and Monsters

10-Minute Plays

"Red Hot and Gold" in *Fool's Gold Anthology '25*, edited by Rebecca Holbourn

"In the Same Boat" in *We/Ourselves: Twenty-Five 10-Minute Plays Celebrating Gender Diversity*, edited by Debbie Lamedman

THE HALF OF IT

DOMENICK SCUDERA

Carnegie Mellon University Press
Pittsburgh 2026

Book design by Connie Amoroso

Library of Congress Control Number 2026937118
ISBN 978-0-88748-749-1

Printed and bound in the United States of America

10 9 8 7 6 5 4 3 2 1

THE HALF OF IT

The Half of It is inspired by the life and work of vaudeville drag artist, Bert Savoy.

CHARACTERS

BERT SAVOY, vaudeville drag performer
JAY BRENNAN, Bert's partner on- and offstage
OHIO, performer friend to Bert
KLONDIKE KATE, the famous "flame dancer" from the Yukon
AGNES, dresser to Savoy & Brennan
MAE WEST, young vaudeville performer
TOUGH, a man cruising other men
ANNIE, Bert's wife
STEVENS, a journalist / theater critic
GREER, a costume designer
HALEY, Bert's roommate
IDA MAY, claims to be Bert's mother

The play can be performed with five actors with doubling. Suggested casting for five actors:

Actor 1: **BERT**
Actor 2: **JAY**
Actor 3: **OHIO / TOUGH / STEVENS / HALEY**
Actor 4: **KATE / AGNES**
Actor 5: **MAE / ANNIE / GREER / IDA MAY**

SETTING

Vaudeville stages and dressing rooms—and the spaces in between. Approximately 1914 to 1923.

ACT 1

Spot on JAY, standing in front of a small vaudeville stage that has its curtain down.

JAY

(To audience:) It was tragic, the ending. That is the whole truth. Tragic. He made headlines across the country the next day. The kind of publicity we had always dreamed of. Well, in our dreams, the story did not include his death, but. . . .

The newspaper described the circumstances this way *(Reading:)* "Long Beach, Long Island, June 27, 1923. . . ."

Curtain opens on the vaudeville stage, revealing BERT and OHIO in bathing costumes. They walk side by side on the beach (created by vaudeville-style moving waves).

"Bert Savoy, well-known comedian of the vaudeville team of Savoy and Brennan"—I'm Brennan, by the way. . . .

BERT

What a glorious day to be alive!

JAY

. . . and that is my Bertie.

BERT

Your Bertie? Dearie, I am my own person. I am Bert Savoy, well-known comedian of the vaudeville team . . .

JAY

(Overlapping:) ". . . vaudeville team of Savoy and Brennan, who starred in *Ziegfeld and the Greenwich Village Follies* several seasons, and Jack B. Grossman, 33 . . ."

OHIO

33! I am not 33 years old.

BERT

Ohio, dearie. The world is bound to find out your true age sometime. Thank god they didn't report my age. That has been a closely guarded secret for many years.

OHIO

And my stage name is Jack Vincent, not Grossman. You'd think they'd at least get that right.

BERT

Yes, but I like "Ohio." A good nickname is . . .

JAY

Please!

BERT

Sorry. Please continue with this terrible tragedy.

JAY

". . . and Jack B. Grossman, 33 . . ."

OHIO

Ugh.

JAY

". . . also widely known in theatrical circles."

BERT

Oh, he is definitely "widely known"—by half the men of New York!

JAY

You're impossible.

BERT

I am dead.

JAY

Not yet. Please let me continue. "Savoy and Grossman . . ."

OHIO

Vincent.

JAY

"Savoy and Vincent were members of a bathing party given by John Haley, another actor."

BERT and OHIO act out some of JAY's narration in the style of a vaudeville routine:

"The actor companions had motored to the beach from Manhattan, leaving the sweltering city early in the afternoon to seek refuge from the heat. They were disporting themselves merrily by plunging into the surf and playing ball on the sands. Savoy and Grossm—Vincent—apparently tired of both forms of amusement, grasped each other's hand, and danced along the water's edge. . . ."

BERT grabs OHIO's hand

BERT

Dance with me, sweetheart.

OHIO

There are hundreds of people watching us, you big nance.

BERT

Shut it, you fairy.

OHIO

Invert.

BERT

Pansy.

OHIO

Muzzler.

BERT

Queer.

OHIO

Queen.

BERT

Good one, Ohio. I like that one. But, come on, dearie, I am, apparently tired of the other forms of amusement.

BERT gives JAY a look to continue with the story.

JAY

"The two men were capering along the edge of the surf, holding each other by the hand, as though they were playing to a real audience."

OHIO

How does one caper, precisely?

BERT

Stop being such a man. Just take your 33-year-old ass and caper with me.

OHIO

There are people watching us.

BERT

That is the idea, dearie. My whole life is built on this. Enjoy it.

JAY

"The two companions were evincing great delight at the white foam swishing against their feet. The storm rose suddenly and raged for about ten minutes."

OHIO

Storm's coming!

BERT

I hate storms. Always have.

They hear thunder, created by a thunder sheet.

Mercy, ain't Miss God cutting up something awful?!

A lightning bolt cutout drops from the flies. BERT and OHIO collapse in a dramatic, over-acted style.

JAY

"The lightning drew down the final curtain on their act."

The curtain falls on the stage.

BERT

(From behind the curtain:) Wait, stop! *(Sticking his head out of the curtain:)* I do not like that. Shall we try a different line? Jay, dearie, feed me the intro again.

JAY

What?

BERT

Give me the lead-up. I have a better line.

JAY

You are dead.

BERT

You said I was not dead.

JAY

Now you are. The lightning struck you dead. And you do not have any more lines.

BERT

You are the one that has insisted on starting at the end. And this is my tragedy, after all. I want to get it right. *(Cues the curtain to be raised again:)* Curtain!

JAY

"The storm rose suddenly and raged for about ten minutes."

BERT

(To OHIO:) Ahem . . .

OHIO

(Realizing he is being cued to play the scene again:) Oh—Storm's coming!

BERT

I hate storms. Always have.

Thunder is created again.

That'll be quite enough out of you, Miss God!—What do you think? Is that better? I like the "Miss God" part at the end of the line. It allows for . . .

JAY

Bertie, please! What difference does it make? You are about to be struck dead by lightning!

BERT

This is my tragic, fantastic death, dearie. I am not going to leave this earth uttering a mundane line of dialogue. Of all people, you should know that I want to work this routine until it is right.

JAY

You are working my nerves, that is for sure.

BERT

Give it a chance. "That'll be quite enough out of you, Miss God."

BERT cues thunder and lightning stage effects. BERT and OHIO are struck dead again.

JAY

"The lightning drew down the final curtain on their act. *(Curtain drops again.)* The two actors had played their last part."

BERT sticks his head out from the curtain once more.

BERT

Oh, yes. That's good.

JAY

This is not an act, Bertie. What actually happened? You cannot rewrite facts to make your own death more palatable and entertaining.

BERT

Why not? I have concocted just about everything else about my life, have I not, dearie?

JAY

Yes, I suppose you have.

BERT

So what is to stop me now from shaping my grand finale into something spectacular?

JAY

You got yourself killed, you idiot. Why were you in the water with a storm overhead? And why were you wearing that giant key around your neck? You were asking to get hit by lightning!

BERT

This is a bathhouse locker key.

JAY

Of course it is.

BERT

What is that supposed to mean? I am not responsible for this tragedy. It was fate. I had a feeling from early that day that something bad was going to happen. As we were leaving the city this morning . . . *(Curtain rises again so he can act out this moment:)* I looked back into the apartment and I said, *(dramatic:)* “I feel like I am never coming back in here again.”

JAY

So dramatic.

OHIO

She really did say that! I was there.

BERT

How was I supposed to stop it? It all happened so fast. And where were you, anyway? My great partner? Why were you not there to protect me?

JAY

You know perfectly well that the doctor sent me to French Lick Springs.

BERT

French Lick Springs? Is that a real place? I have never heard of anywhere so ridiculous.

JAY

The doctor ordered me to go to the springs to rest and settle my case of bad nerves.

BERT

Bad nerves?

JAY

Yes. *You* gave them to me!

OHIO

Ha! I know! She is a handful, this one!

BERT

Will you please be quiet? Or drop dead again. You are not integral to this story.

OHIO

I was killed by a lightning bolt standing next to you. That is integral.

BERT

I needed to get away, too.

JAY

From me?

BERT

Yes. You are not the only one with bad nerves.

JAY

Oh, please. Nothing ever bothers you.

BERT

That is an illusion.

JAY

Your whole life is an illusion.

BERT

I do not believe in illusion. You are just jealous, Jay, dearie.

OHIO

What is going on? You're jealous of what? Me? Oh, no! There is nothing happening between me and . . .

BERT

Of course not, Ohio. I already told you: you are not important to this story.

OHIO

That's right. Wait, what?

JAY

Ohio, do not let your feelings get hurt. He is saying that I am jealous of him and Haley.

OHIO

What's Haley got to do with anything?

BERT

Haley moved in with me. We were living together in my apartment. Jay could never stand the thought of the two of us together.

JAY

You don't know the half of it, dearie.

BERT

That is my line.

JAY

Yes, I know. Your famous line—"You don't know the half of it, dearie." Well, you are dead now, dearie, so I can say and do whatever I want. And I can tell your story however I want.

BERT

And it will not be half as good as I could tell it, dearie. What did the newspapers say? "The lightning drew down the final curtain on their act."

JAY

You cannot trust the newspapers for accuracy.

OHIO

So true. They reported I was 33!

BERT

Shut it, Ohio.

JAY

And for that matter, *you*, dear Bertie, you cannot be trusted for accuracy either.

BERT

Say what you want, but you were devastated when I was gone. You cannot replace me so easily.

JAY

Oh, but I did. After this tragic day, I found myself a new vaudeville partner—within months.

BERT

Yes, and you never reached the same success as you did with me, now, did you? Brennan and Rogers does not have the same zing as Brennan and *Savoy.*

OHIO

Gentlemen, please.

BERT

I am not a gentleman, I will have you know!

OHIO

Lady, gentleman, invert. Whatever. It's time to put all this bickering aside. I may not be important in the scheme of things. But I know that you, Jay, are the one he loves. Don't you let him tell you otherwise. Since the day you two met, there was that energy, that bolt of lightning between you. Sorry—bad choice of words there.

BERT

May I take control of this story, please? After all, this is my life we are sharing, is it not? *(To audience:) The Birth of "Savoy and Brennan"*—version one.

JAY

Version *one*?

BERT

Ohio, help me get out of this bathing costume and into something that fits my story.

OHIO

I thought I wasn't important.

BERT

Oh, you are impossible! Help me dress and I shall set the scene. We must share with this audience the magnificent story of how Jay and I first met and came up with the idea for our act.

OHIO helps BERT change costume as he narrates.

Manhattan. Forty-Second Street and Broadway. Eight years ago: 1915. Morning. Snow is falling. It is cold. Brennan and I had met once or twice prior to this when we happened to play the same theaters. We bump into each other on the street. Thank you, Ohio. You can go.

OHIO

But, I . . .

BERT

Please, honey. You are a sweet friend but, other than the fact that we were fried by lightning together, you are superfluous to my story. Let it not hurt your feelings. Now go.

OHIO hesitates, goes to say something, thinks better of it, and leaves.

JAY

Why do you do that? Why do you push everyone away?

BERT

I do no such thing. Now please act out your part. It is 1915; it is cold; we bump into each other on the street.

BERT and JAY take the stage and act out their first meeting, walking into each other on the street corner. It is played like one of their routines.

Watch where you're going!

JAY

Everett?

BERT

Yes, that's right. Who . . . oh, James! *(Aside, to audience:)* A little side note: we were going by different names then. More about that later.

JAY

It is nice to run into you. Literally. How are you faring these days, old boy? Any good job prospects?

BERT

Nah. Same lousy work I was doing when our paths crossed before. You?

JAY

Nothin'.

BERT

Say, James, what do you say we fix up an act together? We could get us better bookings!

JAY

They couldn't get any worse.

BERT

I can scare up a dress.

JAY

And if we think up our own jokes, our laughs won't cost us nothing!

BERT

Gosh, I believe this could be the start of something big!

JAY

(To audience:) It did not happen like that. We did not simply run into each other and—boom!—an act is born.

BERT

Well, it makes for a good story. It's romantic and, well, encouraging. But if you insist. . . . We can move on to . . . *The Birth of "Savoy and Brennan"*—version two.

JAY

What?

BERT

1915. Manhattan. Summertime. That awful warm part of the summertime. A window ledge in a high rise. I am draped over a window, saying goodbye to a coupla friends—"Goodbye!"—Jay is walkin' by, looking for a butcher shop to get a piece of meat.

JAY

What?!

BERT

Just do it.

JAY

A butcher shop? *(Begrudgingly gets on stage again to play out another routine:)* Anyone know where there is a butcher shop around here?

BERT

Then he sees me.

JAY

Say, we're havin' dinner at our house, mebbe you kin tell me where to get a ham?

BERT

Say, wait a minute. Can you sing?

JAY

Why yes I can!

BERT

Gosh, I'd love to tell you about an act I have in mind. Come on up!

JAY

(Breaking from the storytelling:) Our lives are not a routine. I did not walk down the street asking strangers where to find a ham. Where do you come up with these ridiculous tales?

BERT

I find it inspiring that, when we first saw each other, there was a spark there.

JAY

Or a ham.

BERT

We were connected instantly.

JAY

Were we?

BERT

It would be nice to think that we were. *(JAY gives him a look, annoyed)* Oh, alright. How about this? *The Birth of "Savoy and Brennan"*—version three. 1914. Chicago.

JAY

Now it's 1914? Are we getting younger?

BERT

1914. Chicago. A streetcar.

BERT makes like he is riding on a streetcar

JAY

No. No! There has to be some truth to our lives, Bert.

BERT

No? How about this: 1914. Cleveland. I am understudying for Jim Russell in the Russell Brothers Irish servant-girl act. You happened to catch the show that night and immediately conceived the great possibilities of our act.

JAY

You cannot just make up facts to entertain yourself.

BERT

But I did go on for Jim Russell. The Russell Brothers were the best female impersonators in the business.

JAY

Yes, but . . .

BERT

That is where I refined my girl act on the legitimate stage.

JAY

Legitimate? That offensive Irish servant-girl act?!

BERT

You are just envious that I was so successful at such a young age.

JAY

I am not jealous. Is anything real to you?

BERT

Green is not an attractive color on you, dearie.

JAY

Will you stop? What I am trying to say is that I did not magically lock eyes on you and a new act was miraculously born out of thin air. You cannot make your life something that it is not.

BERT

Why not?

JAY

It cannot be New York or Chicago or Cleveland. 1914 or ’15. Pick one set of facts.

BERT

Why do we have to adhere to one history?

JAY

This conversation is absurd.

BERT

Maybe it is 1914 *and* '15. Snow *and* summer heat. All at the same time.

JAY

Multiple realities do not exist simultaneously.

BERT

Oh? Am I not man *and* woman.

JAY

Man *or* woman. There must be something definitive, Bert.

BERT

No, it is not a necessity, dearie. And that is your problem, is it not?

JAY

Bertie, I will admit that there are elements of truth in some of those versions of your story. But they do not add up the way you have presented them. Our meeting was not stage-worthy. It was a moment in time. Our paths crossed, we both needed work and were ambitious. We were in the right place at the right time, and we hit it off. End of story.

BERT

How mundane you are, Jay Brennan.

JAY

How lunatic you are, Bert Savoy. Or is it Everett McKenzie? Or maybe it is both at the same time?

BERT

Close your mouth and come here.

JAY

No.

BERT

You know I love you. Come here.

JAY

Is this part of your act?

BERT

You are part of my act, silly.

JAY slowly warms up to BERT as he talks.

We did not bicker like this early on. We actually enjoyed being together, remember? On- *and* offstage.

JAY

Everything was so much simpler in those days.

BERT

(To audience:) Vaudeville Circuit, the Early Years—version one.

JAY

No, please. Let me set this one up. And no versions. One whole truth. My memory is clear about those days.

BERT

Be my guest.

JAY

Thank you. *(To audience:)* We were a song-and-dance duo, when we first started. We had these matching costumes back then.

Their costumes are thrown to them from offstage.

C'mon, get dressed.

BERT

Where is Ohio when you need him?

JAY

We can do this ourselves. Just let me talk.

JAY and BERT put on their Society Jesters matching costumes as JAY sets up the scene.

We worked the Sullivan & Considine vaudeville circuit. Traveling around the country. Billings, Montana one week; Spokane, Washington the next. It was a crummy circuit, but the best we could do at the time. This is around 1914 or '15.

BERT

Which is it? '14 or '15? It cannot be both at once, can it?

JAY

Ssssshhh. We had our own song-and-dance act, The Society Jesters.

Music begins to play. During this next section, JAY and BERT perform a simple dance routine onstage as they talk.

We were pretty good, if somewhat average. But we were in love.

BERT

Aw.

JAY

And that made it fun and zany. For so many years, I was so very serious. But Bert made my life adventurous. And so worthwhile.

BERT

That is the nicest thing you have ever said.

Music and dancing stop. Mild applause is heard.

JAY

I miss those days.

BERT

Life was so much easier then. Remember that time Kate dropped in to our dressing room?

JAY

Yes. Now this is a story worth telling. We were in some Podunk town in the Midwest. Christmas Eve, 1914.

We are transported to their backstage dressing room, 1914ish, a small Midwest city on their vaudeville tour. BERT and JAY have just finished their act. They are undressing, getting out of their costumes.

BERT

C'mon, dearie. It's Christmas Eve! Lighten up!

JAY

It is raining. I am miserable. We are in some poor, little town in the sticks. This tour is a bore. What is there to be light about?

BERT

Be merry, you dramatic little pansy! This is no Bore Tour! This is vaudeville, baby! You got jugglers, electrical acts, knife throwers! And, of course, everyone's favorite song-and-dance team.

JAY

And yet, night after night, we play to a handful of unenthusiastic stub holders. And, on top of all of that, it is pouring rain on Christmas Eve.

BERT

So? I hate storms, always have, but life is what you make it, dearie. We can make the holiday whatever we want it to be. Believe me, I have had some miserable Christmas Eves before, and this does not even come close. Come here.

JAY

No.

BERT

Come over.

BERT cozies up to JAY

Give me that mug, James. *(BERT kisses JAY, who is resistant to any fun)* We have a terrific act! We are The Society Jesters! The audience of twelve loved us tonight. And we have each other. What else could you ask for? You have to make your own enjoyment.

JAY

As usual, you are right, Everett.

BERT

Everett—how I hate that name. I sound like a doctor. I am thinking of trying out Bert instead.

JAY

Who is Bert?

BERT

Me. I am Bert. The new me. Does it not have a solid, theatrical ring to it? Bert.

JAY

You would just change your name?

BERT

Why not? I have done it before. I once toured the country as "Madame Veen," palmist and fortune teller. Be who you want to be, dearie. Who should you be? "James" is getting a bit dreary. I think you should be . . . Jay.

JAY

And Jay is so much more of a showstopper?

BERT

Of course. It is fresh, more robust. *Jay.* Now we must come up with good last names. What should yours be? Brawley? Brock? Brennan?

JAY

My last name *is* Brennan.

BERT

Well, then, Jay Brennan it is.

JAY

And Jay Brennan is different than James Brennan how?

BERT

It is so much grander, Jay. *Jay* dearie. *Jay* darling. Mr. *Jay* Brennan. Now for me—I need a good last name.

JAY

McKenzie.

BERT

That is my name now.

JAY

I know.

BERT

I deserve something much grander. I do not feel like a McKenzie. I am not suited to be a McKenzie.

JAY

But I deserve to remain a Brennan?

BERT

What shall it be? Bert Rockefeller? Bert Hudson? Bert Empire? Oh, stop looking like that. I am just having some fun. Give me a smile.

Knock on the door

One minute.

BERT and JAY kiss, this time for real.

JAY

Well, I admit, you do know how to have fun . . . Bert.

BERT

I know. Happy Christmas, Mr. *Jay* Brennan. *(There is another knock on the door. To the person knocking:)* Ten seconds! Unless you want to see this girl in her knickers!

BERT steps behind a folding screen to change into something more suitable. A woman enters. It is KATE.

KATE

Excuse me, I am looking for Maude.

JAY

No Maude here. Do you mean Mollie? She is down the hall.

KATE

No Maude? Of course, there is. I just saw her onstage.

BERT

Kate?!

KATE

Maude!

JAY

Maude?

BERT appears, resplendent in a dressing gown.

BERT

Kate, darling! Kate! Kate! Oh, Jay, do you know who this is?

JAY

Kate?

KATE

Oh, how rude of me. Let me introduce myself. I am Kate Stockdale.

BERT

Stockdale? Jay, this is the famous Klondike Kate! You must have heard of her.

JAY

Oh—yes! The Flame Dancer, right? Everett . . . uh, Bert . . . you never told me you knew a legend like this.

BERT

Kate, this is Jay. Mr. *Jay* Brennan.

KATE

Pleasure.

JAY

All mine.

BERT

Now tell us—what is this legend doing in Nowheresville, USA?

KATE

Chasing another man, honey.

BERT

Jay, this woman has had more men than I have teeth. How many times have you been married now?

KATE

Oh, three or four. Five. I've lost count. Husbands are like peanuts. Have one and move on to the next.

JAY

How do you know, uh, Maude?

KATE

This little ray of sunshine popped up in the Yukon a few years back.

JAY

The Yukon? Everett? I mean, Bert. In the Yukon! Ha!

BERT

Why is that so amusing? I am very hardy, I will have you know.

KATE

I was working a concert hall with a bunch o' gals at the height of the Gold Rush. Well, Maude here, she just fit right in.

BERT

The miners thought I was a fine, big, strapping girl!

KATE

They loved our Maude.

JAY

Maude? I thought it was Madame Veen, palmist and fortune teller.

BERT

That was later, dearie, keep up. Madame Veen was when I was working my way from Denver to Baltimore.

JAY

Denver? Baltimore? Yukon?! Where haven't you been?

KATE

Oh, honey, this girl has been everywhere and done everything! Haha—let me get a look at you! Maude. And Madame Veen! Haha! Who is it now, honey?

BERT

I think it is Bert. But we are reserving judgment on that for now.

KATE

One of a kind. Those miners had never seen anything like this one! I thought *I* was the toast of the town up there, but there was nothing like our Maude!

BERT

And look at me now, a two-bit player in a one-horse town.

KATE

We all have to be somewhere, honey. I had a slow start myself at the Savoy Theatrical Company many years ago. . . .

BERT

Savoy! That's it!

KATE

What is it, honey?

BERT

Jay, what do you think? Savoy? Bert Savoy?! It is grand, yes?

JAY

If you say so.

BERT

Miss Stockdale, you are now speaking to the illustrious Mr. Bert Savoy. Pleased to meet you.

KATE

Charmed! Although I have to say that I'd fancy meeting that Madame Veen, palmist and—what was it?—fortune teller?

BERT

Oh, sweetheart, that was one of my finest creations. *(Grabbing Kate's hand, going into character as Madame Veen with a heavy indistinguishable accent:)* Miss Kate, oh, Miss Kate! I see a great love looming in your future!

KATE

Oh, which one, honey?!

BERT

This man is handsome, very, very handsome. . . .

KATE

They all are. That's my problem.

BERT

. . . and he will bring you great riches.

KATE

I have my own riches. I don't need a man for that.

BERT

Then it is no hardship for you to pay for the services of the famous Madame Veen. For this palm reading, you pay me at least two dollars, yes?

KATE

Oh, that's quite the act, honey.

BERT

(Back to being Bert again:) And get this—while they reached for their wallets to get the money, I pinched their pocket watches. Until I got caught, that is.

KATE

No!

BERT

Yes! In Baltimore. Never go to Baltimore, my dear. Unless it is to die.

JAY

I was born and raised in Baltimore.

BERT

And look how you turned out. Anyway . . . I somehow found myself in that godforsaken city. There I was, in my most beautiful Sarah Bernhardt makeup, telling the judge *(overly dramatic),* "Oh, there is a wild misunderstanding, your most gracious honor! I have been greatly wronged, I have!"

JAY

You said this to a judge? In court?!

BERT

He scowled at me: "Why do you have yourself done up like that?" "Oh," I says, "it's just an eccentricity, your honor." And he says: "90 days!"

KATE

You are making that up!

BERT

Now that, Jay, was one miserable Christmas!

KATE

Maude, how I have missed you!

JAY

And where did "Maude" come from, pray tell?

BERT

Well, I started life as a foundling child, you know, all alone in the world.

JAY

No, I did not know. Is that true?

BERT

All alone. And one Christmas, I find myself in the Bowery. It was a nightmare! No home, no parents, no money. I slept in a packing case.

JAY

Is this the story of Maude or David Copperfield?

BERT

That was my lowliest Christmas. I was ever so despondent. So I shipped out on a cattle boat to London. Oh!—The bustle! The excitement! It was everything I needed! I hung around until I got a super's job in a show called *Cheer, Boys, Cheer*. But I found the going hard as a boy. . . .

JAY

(Sarcastic:) You? No!

BERT

(Gives JAY a look) . . . so I dressed, well, as a girl. And that is when everything turned around for me. I did another show, and a pantomime after that, and so on. I hopped a boat back to New York, with a complete riding outfit I had pilfered from one of the grand dames of a London production. It was Christmas Eve . . .

JAY

Why do all these stories revolve around Christmas?

BERT

. . . and I dressed myself up in a flaming red wig and the riding outfit. I breezed into Steve Brodie's and caused quite a sensation! People asked Steve, "Who is she?" "Dunno," he says, "but let's call her Maude! Like the racehorse!" Can you believe it?!

JAY

No.

KATE

You were always the front-runner, that's for sure!

BERT

Kate, we need you around here. This is such a Bore Tour! We need a little excitement that only the Flame Dancer can bring!

KATE

No, honey, I am just passing through. I am going where the wind takes me. Or the man.

BERT

What man is it now? Not that bartender-turned-theater owner?

KATE

Pantages? No. That was several men ago. I have learned my lessons from the likes of him. Jay, this Pantages was such a louse! We had a legendary love affair, we did, and we were such a success. The miners loved us, and we found "creative" ways to make money . . .

BERT

—or *take* money!—

KATE

. . . from them.

BERT

It was a delicious scandal!

KATE

And it was uproarious fun. I was all set to marry this swindler. Until I found he was swindling *me*! Taking *my* money, with no plans to walk down the aisle ever! Then he secretly marries another woman, skips town, and sends me a letter later to let me know the "good" news.

JAY

Oh my.

KATE

I married a miner after that, but, alas. No gold there either.

BERT

Ha!

KATE

Oh, Maude, why can't I marry you and settle down to life of laughter and adventure?

BERT

I am just too much woman for you to handle, my dear.

KATE

Don't I know it. Jay, you keep your grip on this one and don't let her slip away! She's a treasure, I tell you.

BERT

Say, let's all get ourselves a grand, late Christmas Eve dinner and make the best of this rainy, miserable night.

KATE

I would like nothing better, honey, but I must take my leave of you. We are catching the next train out of here. I just wanted to pop my head in and say hello. And now goodbye. Jay—pleasure.

JAY

A happy Christmas to you.

BERT

(Grandly:) Goodbye, Miss Kate Stockdale.

KATE

The merriest of Christmases to you, Maude . . . I mean, Mr. Bert Savoy!

They laugh. KATE leaves.

JAY

You were arrested in Baltimore?

BERT

Oh, Jay! I've got it! Kate has inspired me!

JAY

Got what?

BERT

We need to ditch this song-and-dance act. No more Society Jesters. We need something original. I could pull out my wig, my gowns. . . .

JAY

A comedy act? You as Maude?

BERT

No. Not Maude.

JAY

Veen?

BERT

No! No. *(Thinking, gets an idea:)* Ansonia! I want a fresh start.

JAY

Ansonia? Where do you come up with these ideas?

BERT

Oh, I am brimming with them, baby.

JAY

And what about me?

BERT

You will be the straight man, Jay.

JAY

Very funny.

BERT

No, I mean, you will feed me the lines for the jokes. Brennan the feeder, with Savoy as the comedy damsel! We are going to be big, dearie. I know it!

JAY

Oh, I love you, you crazy invert. Come here. *(They embrace.)* Happy Christmas, my dear Ansonia! I mean Bert. My Bertie.

They kiss. BERT exits.

And the rest, as they say, was history.

JAY puts on the costume for their new act as he talks to the audience:

We went from being two song-and-dance men to being a man-and-woman comedy team. Bertie was, of course, the woman. And I took on the role of the straight man, or feeder. I set up a question, Bertie answers it and gets a laugh—

Me: "What did the Judge say when you sassed him?"
Bertie: "The Judge said I was a trifle too free and gave me 90 days!"

I got a million of 'em. . . .

NOTE: this next joke section can be trimmed or expanded as needed for Bert's costume change. To expand, audience members can be invited to play the jokes with Jay:

"A girl like you . . . you ought to be thinking about your future."
"I am thinking of my future. I'm going to marry a man with a lot of money."
"What? Would you marry any fool if he had money?"

"Well, I don't know. How much money have you got?"

"I'll have you know that I am not as big a fool as I once was."
"No, have you been on a diet?"

"Hey, I'm starting to think you don't like me. Why is it that you are never home when I phone you?"
"Just lucky, I guess."

"Would a kiss be out of place?"
"Not if you're careful."

"Oh, but wait a minute. I'm married. Do you know what bigamy is?"
"Sure, when you have two wives at one time."
"That's right. Now can you tell me what word means having one wife?"
"Yeah, monotony."

"Tell me, have you lived in New York your whole life?"
"Not yet."

"How far is your house from the station?"
"Only a five-minute walk if you run."

"Do you ever wish that the Good Lord could have made you a man?"
"He probably has, but I haven't found him yet."
"No, I mean, do you ever wish *you* were a man?"
"No. Do you?"

With a good feeder, the comic man—or woman—has three-fourths of the battle won. It is a good feeling, and my personality is suited for it. Let's face it—Bertie is the clown, the bigger personality, the center of attention. But he needs someone to put him there. And that is me.

Our not-so-great vaudeville circuit proved to be the perfect testing ground. We tried out jokes, stole some good lines we heard here and there, and refined our act into a comedy machine.

VOICE-OVER

Ladies and gents, next up: have a laugh with the comedy team, Savoy and Brennan!

BERT enters in drag. Lights up on their comedy routine.

JAY

Say, do you know I met a fellow friend of yours this morning. . . .

BERT

How dare you talk to me. Why, the idea! I haven't given you the least bit of encouragement. Why, a girl ain't safe in the street after three or four in the morning.

JAY

Well, would you like to go for an automobile ride?

BERT

No.

JAY

No?

BERT

I'm just walkin' home from one.

JAY

Say, before we go any further, tell me: are you married or single or what is it?

BERT

Or. *(JAY laughs)* I've been married once too often.

JAY

How often have you been married?

BERT

Once. But I'm not married anymore. I'm not married. It takes up so much time. I'm not married. You must come over.

JAY

Yes. But you have been married recently because I remember reading of your divorce.

BERT

Well, I'm not the only one that ever got a divorce. I just had to get a divorce. I don't go for caveman stuff, dearie. Floors were made to walk on, not to be dragged over.

JAY

Yes, but it didn't last very long, did it?

BERT

Well, I was with him from May to September. I don't see how people can say that. I was with him from May to September.

JAY

And then some other woman took him away from you.

BERT

What do I care? I had the use of him all summer.

JAY

What did you divorce your husband for?

BERT

Two hundred dollars a month.

JAY

You're just the kind of girl I'd like for my wife.

BERT

Well, tell your wife she can't have me.

JAY

I'm not married.

BERT

No? Don't you want to be?

JAY

Well, yes—I've half a mind to get married.

BERT

That's all you need. Say, I had a wonderful dream last night. I dreamt about you!

JAY

You did?!

BERT

I dreamt that you and I were married.

JAY

Were you happy?

BERT

Yes, when I woke up. Say, how old are you?

JAY

Twenty.

BERT

I beg your pardon?

JAY

Twenty, twenty! I said twice . . . twenty!

BERT

Twice twenty, that's better. Well, I must be going.

JAY

Say, what's your hurry? Where are going?

BERT

To a matinee.

JAY

Oh, do you like the motion pictures?

BERT

Yes! Just last week, I went to the matinee. Oh, I'm mad over it. I went to the matinee.

JAY

Just you?

BERT

No, I met a lovely fella in the lobby.

JAY

A lovely fella?

BERT

(Suggestive:) You don't know the half of it, dearie!

JAY

Was he a New York boy or . . . ?

BERT

No, he was a college boy.

JAY

Well, how do you know?

BERT

He had a Yale lock in his pocket.

JAY

You hit it off with him, then?

BERT

Oh, yes. He's the sweetest boy. And he—*he* was good looking.

JAY

Hey, I don't like the way you said that. Certainly you've seen funnier looking men than me, haven't you? Hey, I'm talking to you! You've seen funnier looking fellows than me, haven't you?

BERT

Don't rush me. I'm trying to think.

JAY

Now you don't mean that!

BERT

No, dearie, no. You must come over sometime! You must come over!

Enthusiastic applause. End of routine.

JAY exits. BERT goes to his dressing room. We are backstage at the Ziegfeld Follies, 1918.

BERT

Agnes, dear, help me off with this outfit.

AGNES

Yes, Mr. Savoy. How was tonight's performance?

BERT

I thought last night's opening night was a dream. Tonight was even better! I have not woken up from that dream yet!

AGNES

And Mr. Brennan, is he having fun, too?

BERT

Oh, yes! He is chatting up some newspaper reporter now.

AGNES

Without you?

BERT

He will not allow me to be seen offstage in costume.

AGNES

And you don't mind? Those reporters are here to see you!

BERT

He is focused on creating the right image. He has gotten us where we are today, so I try not to argue too much.

AGNES

You?!

BERT

I want to revel in my happiness. I make no waves tonight. Besides, I received all the attention onstage. He is good with the publicity behind-the-scenes. I cannot argue that.

AGNES

Have you seen these reviews from last night's premiere?! I've been readin' 'em while you were doing your skits. Oh my! You boys are a hit!

BERT

We are not boys, Agnes dear. Well, at least I am not. And I do not lower myself to read reviews. Those reviewers are idiots. But . . . well, just this once. Read a little of one of those raves, won't you?

AGNES

(Reading:) "Wednesday, June 19, 1918. Newest 'Follies' Is Bold and Bountiful. The annual 'Follies' of Florenz Ziegfeld, Jr., was given its premiere performance before an expectant and overflowing house last night. It is a brave, bountiful, and beautiful show this season. . . ."

BERT

Yes, yes, yes. Get to the good part!

AGNES

Let's see . . . here we go! "Above all, Savoy and Brennan are on hand—especially Savoy—whose manner is changeless as the eternal hills but who knows the secret cave where the good jokes are hidden. I was convulsed with mirth, thanks to the efforts of Bert Savoy. The man is priceless . . ."

BERT

A man?! He calls me a man! Ha! Go on. . . .

AGNES

"The man is priceless, and he gets away with blue murder. No one in my box laughed as immoderately as I, and then I realized my own lowbrow vulgar tastes. Mr. Savoy's double enters, double entrers—

BERT

Double entendres.

AGNES

. . . double entendres are unique, and as a female impersonator he stands alone."

BERT

Take that, Julian Eltinge, you fat cow! Ha! I love it! Here, love, help me get this dress off now.

During the next conversation, AGNES helps BERT undress

AGNES

Oh, Mr. Savoy, how do you do it?

BERT

Do what, dearie?

AGNES

Well, you are a good fella. How do you . . . dress yourself up like this—like a lady—and make people laugh so?

BERT

I have been doing it my whole life, Agnes.

AGNES

Making people laugh? Or dressing like a lady?

BERT

Both.

AGNES

Now, don't take this the wrong way, but isn't dressing up in all this finery a bit, well, unusual for a boy? I ain't judgin', don't get me wrong. I am a good Christian woman, and it is not up to me to judge nobody, but most boys wouldn't want to dress like a girl.

BERT

I am not most boys. Let me tell you a story. I was a difficult child, as you can imagine. My mother left, dumped me on my grandmother who sent me off to a very stuffy boarding school. Do not tell Mr. Brennan this—I have never mentioned any of this to him.

AGNES

Oh, I can keep a secret.

BERT

It is not a secret. Not really. Frankly, it is not all that interesting. That is why I have not mentioned it to Jay. It does not fit with my life history, or at least what he believes my life history to be. Anyway, I was dispirited, not the best of students. So I auditioned to be in one of the school theatricals.

AGNES

And that's where you fell in love with the stage!

BERT

No. That was a snooze. I hated it.

AGNES

I would think you would take to the stage like a fish to water.

BERT

I was good at it, but I was better at making fun of our teachers. One day, I grabbed a girl's skirt from the costume closet and threw it over my trousers and started mimicking Mrs. McPhee, our prim mathematics teacher. "Now listen up, children, 2 + 2 = 4!" The boys were falling over themselves with laughter! I was getting the attention I needed—and deserved—so I took it a little further. The next day, I had a wig, glasses, dress—"3 + 3 = 6!" The boys were suffocating from laughing so hard! But then who should walk in but. . . .

AGNES

Mrs. McPhee! Oh my!

BERT

That little shrew reprimanded me. But I kept doing it, making little parodies of all of our teachers. I was a sensation. And . . . sometimes I would dress up outside of school. You know, to keep the limelight on me. But . . . well. . . .

AGNES

What happened?

BERT

I was expelled. My grandmother would have nothing to do with me after that. She was ashamed. I was fourteen.

AGNES

I am sorry, Mr. Savoy.

BERT

I was a big nance from the start, Agnes.

AGNES

Then why do you tell Mr. Brennan all those made-up stories?

BERT

Because I want him to love me, Agnes.

There is a knock on the door.

Agnes, be a dear and see who is at the door while I put something on.

BERT goes behind the dressing screen. AGNES opens the door to reveal MAE.

AGNES

Mr. Savoy is dressing now. May I help you?

MAE

It's okay, darlin'. Let me in. These eyes have seen it all.

BERT appears in a dressing gown.

BERT

Aaah! Mae, baby! Or is it Mary Jane? Or—I heard somewhere that you were using Jane?

They embrace.

MAE

It's Mae, my love. I was born Mary Jane. And Jane is my nom de plume.

BERT

I cannot keep up. It is all so confusing!

MAE

Says Bert / Everett / Veen / Maude / Ansonia . . . shall I continue?

BERT

We are kindred souls, you and I.

MAE

I know it.

BERT

Agnes, let me introduce you to Miss Mae / Jane / Mary Jane.

AGNES

How'd'you do?

MAE

You tell me, honey. I think I am looking fairly spectacular this evening.

BERT

I'll say! It has been too long, honey. When was the last time we saw each other?

MAE

Oh, I can't even remember! *(To AGNES:)* We were old buddies on the vaudeville circuit, Miss Agnes. Our paths crossed here and there when we were out touring the sticks.

BERT

You should have heard the jokes we got away with then, Agnes. *(An old routine:)* "Did I ever tell you the story about the empty box?"

MAE

"You did not. Tell me about it."

BERT

"No use—there's nothing in it."

AGNES

Ha ha! I love it! You know, I once hit the boards myself, another lifetime ago.

BERT

You, Agnes? On the stage? I did not know that.

AGNES

Yes, but illness and . . . a few other mishaps . . . caused me to accept a different position. As dresser to these bananas!

MAE

Aren't you precious?!

AGNES

(Laughs uproariously) I wouldn't trade it for the world! What a life I have! Surrounded by you talented people. Now—let me take my leave of you. I'll take these things to wash and give you two merrymakers time to catch up.

MAE

Pleasure.

AGNES

It is my pleasure, Miss Mae / Mary Jane / Jane!

AGNES laughs and exits

MAE

She is a delight.

BERT

A treasure, absolute treasure.

MAE

Oh, Bertie. How did you do it? You're in Ziegfeld's show, you have a dresser . . . and a handsome partner! Not the same struggling child I remember from the circuit.

BERT

I am all grown up now, dearie.

MAE

Well, I hope that's not true. A serious and mature Bert Savoy would be a sin. You're a "merrymaker," my love. And that act! I laughed my ass off tonight! Did you hear me out in the audience?

BERT

That cackling! That was you?!

MAE

None other. But seriously, Bertie. How did you do it? You've gotten so good. Your timing. Those jokes!

BERT

It's all Jay. He writes the routines. I just say the words.

MAE

No, honey, it's not. It's you. There's something about you. You have "It."

BERT

Well, half of "It," maybe.

MAE

Don't be modest. It isn't like you. C'mon, now, I need to learn how you transformed yourself into, into . . . "It"!

BERT

You do not need help, lovey. You are a force to be reckoned with.

MAE

My career is stalling. Most of my family has disowned me. I need advice. You are so confident now. You're a new woman!

BERT

It is an act. I am not all that confident.

MAE

Ridiculous! That sass, that swagger. Teach me how you do it. I need a new angle in my act. Something fresh.

BERT

I would make a terrible teacher. Besides, you have learned all the lessons you need. You are one of the strongest people I know.

MAE

It's an act.

BERT

We are cut from the same cloth, aren't we?

MAE

You had them eating out of the palm of your hand. *(Mimicking BERT's act:)* "I'm not married. It takes up so much time. I'm not married. You must come over!" Priceless!

BERT

Actually, I have a price. And it has gone up since this show is a hit!

MAE

Tell me how you do it. "You must come over!" Where do you get that from?

BERT

From strong ladies like you, dearie. You just see yourself in me.

MAE

What do you mean?

BERT

You could do this act with your eyes closed, my love. People are just laughing at me because I have the guts to wear a dress and talk about sex.

MAE

But you're not talking about sex. At least not on the surface.

BERT

It's all in the delivery. If the line is clean, you can make the subtext as dirty as you want. It's the audience's minds that are in the gutter, not my mouth. *(Suggestively:)* "Did I ever tell you the story about the . . . empty box?"

MAE

Ha!

BERT

(Dirty:) "There's nothing in it . . . at the moment."

MAE

You are incorrigible!

BERT

You can do it with any line: *(Suggestively:)* "You must come over." Try it—just be yourself and deliver me that line. . . .

MAE

"You must come over."

BERT

Good. But make it your own. Do not imitate. I am not imitating you. Or any woman. I am inspired by you. I am inspired by women. Let it come full circle—be inspired by me.

MAE tries out a walk, a new attitude, while riffing on the line.

MAE

"Oh, you must come over. Come on over, lovey. Oooh, you must come over."

BERT

That's it, that's it.

As she tries out the line, she is growing into the Mae West persona that eventually will make her famous.

MAE

"Why don't you come over? Come over and see me. Why don't you come up? Come up and see me sometime?"

BERT

Oh, baby, you are dangerous!

MAE

You don't know the half of it, dearie!

BERT

Ha! Oh, how I love you!

BERT and MAE embrace. MAE exits as BERT talks to the audience. He dresses to go out.

Is that how Mae West discovered her persona and her famous line? Perhaps. Perhaps not. But, truly, I was inspired by her. She was inspired by me. Underneath the women's clothes, people saw me as a man—and that gave me permission to be audacious, and to say outrageous things. It took another decade before they would accept a woman onstage saying outrageous things. Well, maybe "accept" is not the right word. They arrested Mae a coupla times for it. But she knew the value of a good news story. She exploited those arrests to get her name in the headlines, day after day. She parlayed that persona into a huge career. A career I could only dream of attaining. Alas, a little lightning ruined my rise, but not Mae's.

BERT is now sporting a red necktie. It is late at night. He steps into a dark alley, looking to meet a man. He stands under a streetlamp.

She found what she was looking for. I am still looking.

After a moment, a TOUGH walks by. They glance at each other. TOUGH continues walking as BERT continues watching him.

TOUGH pauses, glances back at BERT again. BERT smiles.

BERT

See something you like, sailor?

TOUGH does not react. He looks around, checking to see that they are alone. He slowly walks back over to BERT. TOUGH stares long at BERT without saying a word. BERT uses a bit from his vaudeville routine to ease the awkwardness:

"How dare you talk to me. Why, the idea! I haven't given you the least bit of encouragement."

TOUGH

What?

BERT

"Why, a girl ain't safe in the street after three or four in the morning."

TOUGH

Shut your trap.

BERT

"Before we go any further, tell me: are you married or single or what is it?"

TOUGH

You talk too much.

BERT

It's a joke, honey. Don't you know who I am? *(No answer.)* "You must come over."

TOUGH grabs BERT hard and pulls him close.

Oooh, rough trade. Well. . . . "I don't go for caveman stuff, dearie. Floors were made to . . ."

TOUGH punches BERT in the face, hitting his left eye. BERT falls to the ground.

TOUGH

Faggot.

BERT staggers to his knees, trying to get up.

What's the matter? Your eye hurts?

BERT

Leave me alone.

TOUGH goes to punch him again. BERT winces. TOUGH stops before hitting him.

Why are you doing this?

TOUGH

You pansies need to be taught a lesson. Let me see that eye.

TOUGH lifts BERT's head to look at his injured eye. While BERT looks at him pleadingly, he kicks him hard in the left eye to increase the injury.

TOUGH has had enough. He walks off, glancing around to make sure that no one has seen them. He turns and looks at BERT one last time before he exits.

And I do know who you are. "You don't know the half of it, dearie."

TOUGH exits. BERT slowly gets up, holding his face. He staggers off.

JAY enters, talks to audience:

JAY

It was not easy keeping that one out of the papers. Bertie almost lost his eye but, not surprisingly, he refused to talk about it. I tried to write some jokes to make light of the situation:

Uses the stage, as if sharing a routine with an audience:

"When I marry I'll marry a candy woman. Why, you ask? Well, if I don't like her I can lick her."

Har har har. No? It ain't easy writing jokes about abuse.

Him: "Does your husband miss you when you are away from home?"
Her: "No; but he frequently misses me when I'm at home."
Him: "How's that?"
Her: "His aim ain't accurate."

I've got a million of 'em.

Him: "Does your husband ever send for you if you happen to stay out late?"
Her: "No, he waits until I get home, then he goes for me."

Ha ha ha.

Vaudeville audiences ate up routines like this. Punching a lady is apparently funny, funny business. No? You don't agree? How about this one. . . .

"I'm going out drinking."
"Why is that?"
"Oh, last night I came home, and I threw an axe at the wife and missed her."
"Gee, you should cut out liquor, if that's the way you carry on."
"I'll have to cut it out; it's spoiling my aim."

No? Here's another one. . . .

"Say, why'd you kick your wife while she was down?"

"She started to get back up!"

If you find that offensive, we can turn the tables and make the man the victim. . . .

"I guess your wife made a deep impression on you."
"Oh, yes, twice."
"Twice?"
"Yes, once when we first met and another time she hit me on the head with a rolling pin."

Still, beating up the lady can receive twice the laughter. A little violent, scandalous behavior is just what audiences want. But. . . .

Turns out we didn't need the jokes. Bertie just added a big floppy hat to cover the left side of his face and—voilà!—she is back onstage again as if nothing ever happened.

BERT enters in drag with hat over the left side of the face, performing:

BERT

"You must come over sometime! You must come over!"

Applause as curtain drops on the stage. BERT and JAY move to a backstage dressing room. It is 1921. Chicago.

BERT

That applause! They love us! Chicago is just what the doctor ordered!

JAY

That's because you made a scandal of things in New York.

BERT

What? I am a hit in New York!

JAY

No. You got hit in New York.

BERT

We are the darlings of Broadway! Look at us—headliners of the best tour in the country!

JAY

Then why are you embarrassing us every minute you are not on the stage?

BERT

What is that supposed to mean?

JAY

Eyes are on us now, Bertie. You are not just another fairy walking Vaseline Alley.

BERT

I will have you know that I am seen with the best of society at Gilhooley's and Monte Carlo. I know how to hobnob with the finest.

JAY

Perhaps. But you also walk around town sporting a red necktie. It is dangerous.

BERT

Oh, I can take care of myself.

JAY

You were beaten to a pulp, Bertie.

BERT

I have erased that sorry episode from my memory.

JAY

And you continue to walk around town in a red necktie! Have you learned nothing?

BERT

What is so shocking about a red necktie?

JAY

If you want to announce to the world that you are a fairy or an invert or whatever you are, I guess it is not a problem.

BERT

It is simply a red necktie, dearie. Nothing more. Onstage, I am wearing a gown, earrings, and heels. Do you not think that audiences get the idea?

JAY

That is an act. It is not real life.

BERT

I am not one person onstage and a different person when I am off.

JAY

It is a game we must play, Bertie.

BERT

You might be playing a game. I am living my life.

JAY

We are becoming well-known. You cannot just flaunt yourself and look for men in the Bowery without repercussions.

BERT

I am the Toast of the Twenties! I am a foundling child who has become the center of society. Horatio Alger could not have written a better story!

JAY

You are a Society Jester and always will be, Bertie. You might be eating steak at Monte Carlo at eight, but by midnight, you're out walking the Fruited Plain looking for some jocker.

BERT

You are jealous.

JAY

No, Bertie. No. I can put up with your occasional dalliances. This is different. This is not our personal lives I am talking about. I am trying to maintain our professional reputation.

BERT

Our reputation is superb! We are headliners! Exactly what we have always wanted!

JAY

Yes, in terms of our professional lives, this is what I have wanted. And I am not going to let you louse it up because you refuse to be responsible.

BERT

What do you want me to do? I am not Julian Eltinge, that fat cow. I am not going to play a woman onstage and then pretend that I am a manly man offstage.

JAY

Eltinge is one of the most successful female impersonators this country has ever known.

BERT

And one of the most miserable people you would ever want to meet. She is a big queen on- *and* offstage, honey, no matter who she is trying to impress. I will not do that. I am not creating an illusion. It is not an impersonation. I am trying to make people laugh. And I am trying to make my life something worthwhile. And you, my dear, are fighting me tooth and nail the entire time. I thought you were supposed to love me.

JAY

Bertie, please, that is not what I am saying. . . .

There is a knock on the door

Not now, please. We are busy.

ANNIE

I wanna see Bert Savoy.

JAY

Not now.

ANNIE

Tell him it's Anna.

BERT

Oh my god.

JAY

Anna?

BERT

Annie?

ANNIE

Let me in.

JAY

Who is it?

BERT does not respond

Who is it, Bertie?

BERT

Someone from my past.

JAY

Who? Who?

BERT

You sound like an owl, dearie.

JAY

Don't joke. Who is it?

BERT

Uh . . . let's just say . . . family.

JAY

What? A sister?

BERT

No.

JAY

Mother?

BERT

No. I told you I am an orphan.

JAY

Well, who is she?

BERT

My . . . wife. Former wife. Whatever.

JAY is left dumbfounded.

ANNIE

Let me in! I got a right!

BERT walks to the door and opens it to reveal ANNIE.

ANNIE

About time. Let me look at you. My god, Bert.

BERT

Um, Annie, this is Jay.

JAY

Jay Brennan. How'd you do?

ANNIE

Anna Savoy. Pleasure.

JAY

Savoy? Anna *Savoy*?

ANNIE

Yes. I'm his wife.

BERT

Former wife.

ANNIE

Didn't the louse tell ya?

JAY

He mentioned it. Recently. But he did not mention that your name was Savoy. How can that be? When were you married?

ANNIE

A million years ago. We was kids.

JAY

But his name was McKenzie then.

ANNIE

Nope. Savoy. Bert Savoy. You know we toured a bit, the two of us did. "Savoy and Savoy." We was pretty good. But we got into some trouble, and we abandoned the act. And this one—well, he abandoned me.

JAY

Savoy and Savoy? *(To BERT:)* You invented that name when Kate came to visit when we first started *our* act. You were not Bert Savoy before that moment.

BERT

Well, maybe I was. Is it really that important, Jay?

JAY

You lied to me.

BERT

I was reinventing myself, dearie. That is hardly what I would call lying.

JAY

You hypocrite!

BERT

I am merely an actor, Jay. Did you know that "hypokrites" was the ancient Greek word for "actor"?

JAY

Unbelievable. I cannot believe a word you say.

ANNIE

Are you his, uh, you know, his. . . . ?

JAY

We are a team. Or so I thought. Did you see our act?

ANNIE

No, I know that. I mean . . . you know.

BERT

Yes, Annie. Yes. Are you satisfied?

ANNIE

I don't give a fig about what you two do.

BERT

Then why ask? And why are you here? I thought you wanted nothing to do with me. I gave you a divorce last year.

JAY

You what?! When did you do that?

BERT

When I took that trip last year. Remember?

JAY

Married. Divorced. Who are you?

BERT

Please, Jay, not now. Annie, why are you here?

ANNIE

I divorced you too soon. I want to get married again.

JAY

You what?!

BERT

Jay, stop. Annie, what are you talking about?

ANNIE

I sees how successful you is in New York City since we got that divorce. You are famous now, ain't ya? Now that you got some good dough coming in, I think it's time your wife started sharing in some of that profit.

BERT

Former wife.

ANNIE

Not if you marry me again. I'll sue you in court, I will. I'll tell them you promised to marry me again and then you disappeared.

BERT

You can't be serious?

ANNIE

Why not? I figure I'm owed somethin'. I'll tell them you got arrested all those years ago.

JAY

In Baltimore?

ANNIE

No. Here in Chicago. It was—I don't know—1906 or 1907.

JAY

You were arrested more than once?

BERT

It was nothing. We got caught receiving some goods.

ANNIE

Stolen goods.

BERT

Oh, it is hardly worth mentioning. We were out in no time.

ANNIE

Yes, but in those fancy New York papers, it would be a scandal. If I leak the truth.

BERT

You were arrested, too, Annie. You are not the most reliable source of information.

ANNIE

I want what is owed to me. And I will figure out some angle that works for me until I get it.

BERT

I am giving you nothing. You know our marriage was not real. We had an act, you wanted us to look legitimate, you talked me into walking down the aisle. But the act faded, I moved on. A dozen years later, you pressure me for a divorce. And now you want to marry me again?

ANNIE

Being married to you is just as big a joke as your act, honey. But, if that's what it's gonna take to make me some money that's owed me. . . .

BERT

I am not going to marry you again, Annie.

ANNIE

Then I'll need a good amount of money to keep myself quiet.

BERT

Excuse me?

ANNIE

You heard me. I'll create a new scandal and then you see how you like it!

BERT

Annie, please, be reasonable.

ANNIE

I'm sorry you have to witness this, Jay. You seem like a nice enough fella. But, Bert here. He was *(suddenly playing the victim, dramatically)* the most abusive husband. Oh yes!

JAY

(Laughing) He was what?

ANNIE

Oh my, yes. A brute.

BERT

Darling, no one is going to believe that.

ANNIE

And why not? The world don't know what you are for real. They sees some refined lady onstage trying to get a yock from an audience. No one knows what's going on when you take that dress off.

BERT

No one will believe I am a tough guy offstage. You were not married to Julian Eltinge. He jumps in a boxing ring to prove how manly he is. You were married to *me*, Annie. I walk around New York in a red necktie.

JAY

Now the necktie is a badge of honor?!

BERT

Please, James, let me handle this.

JAY

And now it's James again?

ANNIE

I thought it was Jay.

JAY

It is. Bertie, this is serious. This woman . . . *(JAY stops abruptly as a thought pops into his head)*

BERT

What is it?

JAY

That's it!

BERT

What's it?

JAY

Think. This could work.

BERT

This is not negotiable. Annie, you have to . . .

JAY

Anna, do you want to go through with this?

ANNIE

Oh, I ain't foolin'!

JAY

Let her do it.

BERT

What?!

JAY

Don't you see?

BERT

No, I don't.

JAY

We'll use the publicity to prove your manliness. Like Eltinge. We can make you a brute offstage . . .

BERT

I am not . . .

JAY

. . . to prove your incredible artistry and illusion onstage. It is brilliant!

BERT

It is not . . .

JAY

Think of it as *Bert Savoy Offstage*—version two. We can throw the focus off of your real New York scandals and play up this angle. And we'll give Anna here a little dough to sing to the papers about what a caveman you are!

BERT

No. I will not do this.

JAY

C'mon, Bertie, you are an actor. A "hypokrite," yes?!

BERT

This is not a joke, Jay.

JAY

Oh, Bertie, I could not have written anything better than this. This is perfect. Anna, let me help you. I am the writer for our little duo. Let me write some dialogue for you. We will make this a love triangle—you, Bert the woman, and Bert the brute!

ANNIE

I knew I liked you, Mr. Brennan. What a mind you have!

JAY

(To audience:) And that's what we did. It took some convincing, but eventually Bertie came around. He was in a corner, and there was no way out. The "scandal" hit the papers in no time. And not just the New York papers. Bert Savoy the Brute made headlines across the country:

December, 1921. "Love Calamities of the Caveman Who Is a Perfect Lady: Whoever heard of a man who is a professional 'lady' blacking his little wife's eyes and walloping the daylights out of her?! Bert Savoy, famous female impersonator, makes us guffaw heartily when onstage. Who would imagine that he is a rough person offstage!"

Curtain up on stage to reveal Anna, acting as tragic heroine:

"Mrs. Anna Clamper Savoy, his wife, says:"

ANNIE

(Playing the victim:) "I treated him kindly and affectionately, as a wife should treat her husband. But soon after we were married, he would come home drunk and beat me! Why, just a few years ago, he gave me a pair of black eyes! I went to a picture show with a girlfriend. He came home and asked me . . ."

BERT is not playing along with this fantasy.

JAY

C'mon, Bertie. Feed it to him again, Anna.

ANNIE

"He came home and asked me . . ."

BERT

(Reluctantly playing out this story:) "Where have you been?"

ANNIE

"To the picture show."

BERT

"I know that because I was sitting right behind you!"

ANNIE

"Well, is there anything wrong about that?"

BERT

"I don't want you to go unless I tell you you can!"

ANNIE

"And he got angry and belted me in the mouth as hard as he could!"

BERT goes to hit her and then breaks out of the "scene."

BERT

This is outrageous. No one in their right mind would believe. . . .

JAY

Bertie, truth is not important here. Saving our act is. *(Continuing the story:)* "Now Mrs. Savoy, nursing a lacerated heart instead of a bruised eye, wants $25,000."

JAY gives some money to ANNIE as he continues:

"And Mr. Savoy, hiding his truth beneath a gorgeous gown, is telling his public every night:"

BERT

"You don't know the half of it, dearie; you don't know the half of it!"

Curtain drops.

JAY

My Bertie was right all along. You can make your own truth. And, if it sells newspapers, you can get them to print just about anything.

ANNIE

Thank you, boys, it is a pleasure doing business with you.

JAY

I will have you know, my good woman, that this is no boy. This is the famous Savoy of the comedy act, Savoy and Brennan!

ANNIE

Goodbye, Bertie.

ANNIE kisses BERT on the cheek. He has no response. She exits.

JAY

C'mon, Bertie, smile. This is the kind of publicity you always wanted!

BERT

I wanted to make headlines for something reputable, Jay. A smash show, a great review, something funny I said. Like that. Not this.

JAY

Trust me, this is a good thing for our careers. We are going to sell tickets like mad after this! They will be clamoring to see you! Be happy! Are you not happy?

JAY kisses BERT. Again, BERT is unresponsive. JAY exits.

BERT, alone. Thunder is heard in the distance.

Blackout. End of Act 1.

ACT 2

New York, 1922. Lights up on BERT and JAY talking to reporter STEVENS backstage in their dressing room. BERT is at a dressing table, talking as he readies himself.

BERT

The theater is becoming too blasé for actor folk, so it requires lots of pepper.

STEVENS

Interesting. Please, go on.

BERT

Some accuse us of being vulgar and common, but just the same, the audience roars with laughter.

JAY

(To audience:) After the marriage scandal played so well and sold so many tickets, Bertie started to enjoy working the press. He became as theatrical and grandiose offstage as he was on. He saw it as another opportunity to perform.

BERT

If ever there was a time when I felt like letting down my hair and being the woman I oughtn't to be, this is the season.

JAY

But, at the same time, we do not want to get in trouble with a censor.

BERT

A censor?

JAY

Yes, you know. A censor is a man who sees three meanings in a joke that has only two. *(To audience:)* I could perform for the press, too, on occasion.

BERT

That's a good line, Jay. Weave it into the next act, old boy. All I know is that the more risqué the joke, the harder the audience laughs. You must walk a fine line. The woman I represent can't be too openly abandoned. She knows everything and knows nothing; wants to make you believe how bad she is and never gives herself a chance to be bad—laughs herself out of it. I'm that way myself; I never have what you would call a perfectly good time—I always talk myself out of it.

JAY

You weren't always like that.

BERT

But there's such a thing as being too conservative. A poor girl must pay her rent!

STEVENS

You are a gem. Tell me, how do you come up with all of your hilarity?

BERT

Jay. Jay is really the brains of the team. He writes all the jokes, thinks them up, and works out all the sketches. We used to sing and dance when we first teamed together, and only used the jokes to fill out, but the public refused to let us go on with the dancing, and we had to cut it out.

JAY

It didn't quite happen that way.

BERT

(Ignoring him; continuing:) They only want to hear us talk, and now they absolutely refuse to listen unless we spring a lot of new ones on them all the time. Oh, it's a dog's life, dearie! It's a dog's life! I wish, I just wish they would take us seriously. Oh, did we mention that we are going to publish a book in the fall titled *The Mutterings of*

Margie? Margie is just the grandest character, she's too funny—she's just too funny for words. You know, it's all about Margie—what she does and says at breakfast, at the matinee, while shopping, or at dinner. Thank goodness for Margie—she is paying our bills, that gal! Isn't that right, Jay?

JAY

Oh, yes. Oh, look at the time. We must get ourselves ready. Thank you so much for coming.

STEVENS

You two are real prizes, I tell you. Thank you! Thank you!

STEVENS exits. As BERT talks to audience, AGNES enters and helps BERT on with wig and hat.

BERT

(To audience:) You are most likely wondering who this Margie is. Margie is the reason for our true success. Once we added her to our act, there was no stopping us.

JAY

Margie does not exist in real life.

BERT

Oh, but she does! Well, she does not actually live and breathe, but she is as true to me as anyone else living! You see, Margie became the society woman that was always making blunders, and I talk about her endlessly in our act.

JAY

Audiences love her. They demand more and more stories about our Margie.

BERT

The idea for Margie was mine. She came to me one day when I was with our dear Agnes. . . .

Lights shift to another moment in the past when AGNES is helping BERT on with wig and hat.

AGNES

Oh, this new hat is just lovely. My friend Mary has one just like it. Well, not quite as nice as this, but she does try to stay up on all the latest fashions. Maybe a year after everyone else, but she gets there eventually!

BERT

Oh, you are bad, Agnes, you are.

AGNES

I love Mary. She does make me laugh. I saw her on the street the other day, and she was on her way to the dentist. Now, keep in mind, this girl has an enormous mouth, so she says, "That dentist is going to get rich off of me!" Oh, she does make me laugh, that girl.

Lights back to original dressing room moment. AGNES has finished helping and exits.

BERT

(To audience:) And Mary made me laugh, too. I told Jay about her. And then Mary became Margie, Margie became the center of our act, and soon we created new adventures for our Margie . . .

JAY

. . . and the act began to write itself.

VOICE-OVER

We know you've been wondering what has happened to Margie this week. Let's find out! Ladies and gentlemen, please welcome Savoy and Brennan!

BERT and JAY step onto the stage and perform their latest routine:

JAY

Say, I'm glad I ran into you. I heard your friend Margie got into some trouble up there on 65th Street. Is that right?

BERT

Wasn't that terrible? Wasn't that awful?

JAY

What happened?

BERT

Everybody in that building lost something. Everybody in that place lost something.

JAY

Well, did they suspect her?

BERT

I say nothing. My lips are sealed. But poor Marge, she was arrested.

JAY

No, don't tell me!

BERT

And I'll never forget, if I live to be a hundred, I'll never forget when she got in front of the judge.

JAY

Why, what's the matter?

BERT

The judge asked Marge if she was the defendant. He asked her if she was the defendant.

JAY

Yes. Go on. The judge asked her if she was the defendant, and what did she say?

BERT

"No. I'm the woman who stole the stuff."

JAY

You know, I met her on the street the other day, and she's going to the dentist. She said she was going to have a plate put in her mouth.

BERT

She's going to have a plate put in her mouth?

JAY

Uh huh.

BERT

It's big enough for a platter.

JAY

I know. But she'd be a nice looking girl if it wasn't for her teeth.

BERT

Isn't it too bad? Poor Marge. She's always going to dentists.

JAY

Yes?

BERT

I'll never forget one time I went to the dentist with her, and the dentist wanted to give her gas.

JAY

Yes?

BERT

He says, "Do you want gas?" and Margie, she says, "Yes, and see how my oil is, too."

JAY

Is Margie married?

BERT

No, she's a widow.

JAY

Where did she bury her husband?

BERT

She said his last wish was to be buried in San Francisco, but Margie buried him over in Brooklyn.

JAY

But she should have carried out his wish.

BERT

That's what his sister said: "If you don't he's liable to come back and haunt you." I thought I'd die! Margie said, "We'll try him over in Brooklyn. If he bothers me, I will send him to 'Frisco."

JAY

Oh my.

BERT

That ain't the half of it, dearie, not the half of it. Margie wanted to talk with her dead husband, so we went to see a medium. A medium who could see through anything!

JAY

Anything?

BERT

That's right, she could see through anything. And Margie ran right out of the room.

JAY

She did?

BERT

I says, "Marge, why'd you run out?" and she says, "I have on a one-piece dress!"

JAY

No?!

BERT

Oh, yes!

JAY

You and Margie make quite the pair.

BERT

If we ruled the world, we would make it compulsory that all women should bob their hair; then the earth would be a charming place on which to live.

JAY

I should say so!

BERT

That's why Margie went out and got herself a curling iron and some carbolic acid.

JAY

Huh?

BERT

Yes, she wants to curl up and dye.

JAY

Now that's sophisticated!

BERT

Oh, yes!

JAY

(Laughs) Say, you two sophisticated gals must have had a wonderful trip to Europe last year. . . .

BERT

Oh, I'm glad, I'm glad you asked me.

JAY

It must have been thrilling.

BERT

Oh, you don't know the half of it, dearie. You don't know the half of it.

JAY

Tell me of some of your experiences.

BERT

Oh, listen, you know, one night when we were out on the ocean, the ship stopped!

JAY

Yes?

BERT

Marge said, "What's the matter?" And the captain said the rudders broke. And I'll never forget Margie's response.

JAY

Go on. The captain said the rudders broke. What did Margie say?

BERT

Margie says, "That's alright. It's underneath. Nobody will notice it." *(Laughs.)*

JAY

I bet you had lots and lots of fun on deck.

BERT

Oh, every night, we'd get on deck and tell stories.

JAY

Yes?

BERT

And, you know, the captain told us about a man who once took his wife out in a boat and threw her overboard.

JAY

Well, he was a brute!

BERT

He said every time she come up, he'd hit her head with an oar. Every time she come up, he hit her.

JAY

Oh my.

BERT

I'll never forget Margie! I'll never forget what Margie said to that!

JAY

Hold on. Every time she came up, he'd hit her over the head with the oar. And what did Margie say?

BERT

Margie says she was a fool to come up! *(Laughs.)*

JAY

I bet you met lots of interesting people on the boat.

BERT

Yes, but Marge ruined the whole party. She ruined the whole party.

JAY

How did she do it?

BERT

Sunday morning, she was playing a rag on the piano in the music room.

JAY

She should have known better.

BERT

And some minister said, "Miss, don't you know the ten commandments?"

JAY

And?

BERT

Margie says, whistle the first three or four bars, and I'll follow you. *(Laughs.)*

JAY

Well, uh, did you get seasick?

BERT

I didn't, but Margie did.

JAY

Well, I sympathize.

BERT

Oh, I felt sorry for her.

JAY

Oh.

BERT

Oh, they gave her everything but the anchor to keep her quiet.

JAY

Well, no wonder. . . .

BERT

Oh, when we got off the boat, they had to take a taxi. Everybody thought she'd been drinkin'. Heaven knows, she just had a few harmless nips. A few harmless nips.

JAY

Well, what made them think she was drinking?

BERT

Well, she stepped in one door of the taxi and fell out the other. *(Laughs.)*

JAY

And?

BERT

And she says, "How much do I owe ya?"

JAY

No! You don't say?!

BERT

Ha ha! Yes! Ain't it the truth?! Ain't it grand? It's grand. It is just grand.

Big applause.

BERT and JAY move to the dressing room. They are joined by AGNES.

What a glorious audience, do you not agree, Jay, dear? Oh, Agnes, take this shawl. I have torn it again. These costumes are becoming so threadbare. The public should not see me if I do not look my best. See what you can do, dear, will you not?

AGNES

Of course, Mr. Savoy. Speaking of costumes, the designer you asked to see is here to meet with you.

BERT

Perfect timing! I need some new frocks desperately!

AGNES

I'll send her in.

AGNES exits.

BERT

Jay, be a love and fade. A lady would like a little privacy.

JAY

Don't be ridiculous. Since when are you so modest?

BERT

Let me have a little time alone with this girl. I want to make sure she has my undivided attention.

JAY

But I. . . .

BERT

Go talk to the manager about that dog act. How can I prepare to go onstage when all I hear is that yip-yip-yipping? Go on, now.

GREER appears at the door.

GREER

Mr. Savoy?

JAY

She is right here. And she is all yours. Enjoy.

JAY exits as GREER enters dressing room.

GREER

Mr. Savoy?

BERT

Miss Greer, is it?

GREER

Yes, that's right.

BERT

Well, come in, dearie, don't be shy!

GREER

What a distinct pleasure it is to meet you! *(Enthusiastically shakes BERT's hand)* May I say what an honor it is to design some costumes for you! I believe there has never been a greater comedian and female impersonator combined to walk the footlights than you, sir. Or should I say madam?! *(Awkwardly laughs at her own joke.)*

BERT

Yes, well, thank you.

GREER

And may I say that I am thrilled that you are giving this opportunity to a woman designer? I realize that there are so many more illustrious male designers whom you could have chosen.

BERT

I contend that it takes a woman to understand a woman's clothes.

GREER

Oh yes!

BERT

Let us get down to business, shall we? What do you have to show me?

GREER

Straight to work! Yes! That's what I like—a truer professional I don't believe I've ever met. . . .

BERT

Miss Greer.

GREER

Right. I apologize—I am a bit nervous.

BERT

You are not afraid of me, dear, are you? That nonsense that was in the papers last year saying that I was a caveman and a brute—you don't believe any of that, now do you?

GREER

Oh no! I am just a bit flustered because I want to do a good job for you, Mr. Savoy. So, um . . . I have made some sketches for you, Mr. Savoy.

BERT

Bert, please.

GREER

Yes. Bert. You can see in this first one that I have created something that I believe is quite dashing. The skirt has a beautiful sweep to it, and the hat is at an angle that is ever so fetching.

BERT

The hat is angled down over the right eye, yes?

GREER

Yes. That's how I've drawn it here. Is that a problem?

BERT

I always wear my chapeaux to drape over my left eye. You see, I am somewhat blind in that eye.

GREER

Oh, I hadn't noticed.

BERT

Some believe I have a glass eye, but that is bunk.

GREER

May I ask what happened to your eye—Bert?

BERT

You may ask, but I will not tell you. A lady must keep certain secrets.

GREER

Oh, yes, of course. I understand. I'll just make a note—hat, left eye—got it.

BERT

And the hat. Not just one or two feathers, now. I want a cascade, a waterfall of feathers.

GREER

Yes. Lovely. *(Writing it down:)* Cascade, waterfall, feathers, left side. . . .

BERT

What else have you got to show me?

GREER

I'm particularly excited to show you this one. I would like to suggest to you a dress with a collapsible bustle, which could come off during your number. I believe this would add to the laughter that you are building—

BERT

Miss Greer, no! Humor is not something I want in my clothes!

GREER

No humor in your clothes?

BERT

Absolutely not. I want to be chic in appearance. Let the ribaldry come from inside.

GREER

Yes, I see!

BERT

For the same reason, I never remove my wig on stage.

GREER

Your signature red bob!

BERT

That is correct. I am creating a character, and I do not want to ruin it by showing the audience this balding head. Without my wig, my chic apparel, my makeup—I look like your average president of a bank. We do not want that now, do we?

GREER

No, no, we would not.

BERT

My gowns must be the richest of fabrics, with vivid dyes and hues—the highly colored garb of a newly rich woman! Have you even seen my act?

GREER

Many times! Yes! I simply thought that. . . .

BERT

Miss Greer, your sketches here are fetching, but if we are to work together, we must be of the same mind.

GREER

Oh, of course, of course. Let me just jot this down—chic, attractive, hat on the left. . . .

BERT

I believe you have already written that down.

GREER

Yes, of course, of course! Please excuse me, Mr. Savoy, uh, Bert. It's just that I wanted so to impress you.

BERT

No need, dear girl. I give you my approval. Sew up this first one you have designed, and we will take it from there. With the hat to the left.

GREER

Yes, yes! Right away. Thank you, Bert. Thank you for this opportunity. I'll have to take a few measurements, if I may.

BERT

Yes, but I must ask you to be quick about it. I have a busy afternoon.

GREER

Of course, of course.

GREER takes out a measuring tape and starts to take some measurements. Throughout the next exchange, she is measuring and writing down notes.

BERT

How long have you been doing this, Miss Greer?

GREER

Oh, please, Mr. Bert, please call me Harriet.

BERT

Harriet, yes. Have you been at this long?

GREER

Not too long, sir. But I am working my way up.

BERT

Are you now? How is the costume business these days?

GREER

There is quite an explosion of shows lately. The opportunities are there if you work hard enough. And if someone will give a lady a chance.

BERT

And do you work hard, Harriet?

GREER

Yes. Oh my yes.

BERT

I see. You know I worked hard, too. But that is not what got me ahead in this business.

GREER

No?

BERT

I started as a cooch dancer in a freak museum in Boston.

GREER

You? A cooch girl? Really?

BERT

Are you scandalized?! Ha ha! We all have to start someplace. Even if it is as a taxi dancer for lecherous male patrons. Anyway, Jay—Mr. Brennan—he says I should never reveal my past because it might embarrass the act. But the truth is the truth. Correct, Miss Greer—Harriet?

GREER

Truth, yes.

BERT

And I am not embarrassed. I performed twelve times a day for six dollars a week. I was doing quite well. I alternated with a deaf-mute girl. She and I were doing so well, we teamed up and joined a carnival. But then the owner skipped with the gate and left us flat without a nickel to get back home on. The shock was so great that, when I informed the deaf-mute of the calamity, it restored her voice, and she uttered, "Oh, my gawd!"

What's the matter, dear? Why have you stopped?

GREER

I must measure the inseam. But I don't want you to think I am being improper.

BERT

Be bold, honey. It is not a problem. Put your hand right up there. What I have between my legs is really of no importance. I have nothing to hide.

GREER

I've got it. Thank you.

BERT

Now, where were we?

GREER

Deaf-mute girl. Rough life.

BERT

Rough, yes. But life was exciting back then, too. I played honky-tonks all across America. Just drifting, performing. I even ended up in the Yukon for a spell.

GREER

Searching for gold?

BERT

Something like that. I miss it. I do.

GREER is finishing up with the measurements.

GREER

But look how you've succeeded! You are Savoy of Savoy and Brennan! Gosh!

BERT

Yes, but it was so much easier then. Now I have everyone telling me how to live my life, what I must and must not do. People don't tell you what to do, do they, Harriet?

GREER

Well. . . .

BERT

Listen, you just get that outfit made for me. Remember—cascade, left side, chic. If I use it in the act, I will commission another gown from you straight away.

GREER

Yes, thank you.

BERT

And when it is ready, you must come over.

GREER

Come over, yes.

BERT

That is a line from the act, dear. "You must come over." You did say that you have seen the act, did you not?

GREER

Oh, yes! Yes! Alrighty, then. Thank you, sir, I mean Mr. Sav—Bert. I will, um, "come over" . . . when the dress is ready.

BERT

Thank you, Harriet. Oh, and be a dear, see if you can round me up a cup of coffee or something before you leave. Thank you.

Scene shifts to nighttime. It is after-hours in the theater. BERT steps onto the empty stage, with a script in his hands. He is privately rehearsing Viola's monologue from Twelfth Night*:*

BERT

Disguise, I see, thou art a wickedness,
Wherein the pregnant enemy does much.
How easy is it for the proper-false
In women's waxen hearts to set their forms!
Alas, our frailty is the cause, not we!
For such as we are made of, such we be.
How will this fadge? my master loves her dearly;
And I, poor monster, fond as much on him;
And she, mistaken, seems to dote on me.

AGNES has entered and is watching from the wings. BERT notices her.

Agnes! You frightened me!

AGNES

My apologies.

BERT

Is there something you wanted?

AGNES

You are quite good.

BERT

Pardon?

AGNES

Viola. *Twelfth Night.* You're good.

BERT

Thank you, Agnes. Mr. Brennan laughs at my Shakespearean aspirations. At least someone appreciates me.

AGNES

It's rather fitting.

BERT

What is?

AGNES

Well, you—a man—playing a woman's role. And that woman is playing a man's role!

BERT

It sounds confusing. But I can relate.

AGNES

Shakespeare's men performed all the roles in his day. You are bringing back an honored tradition!

BERT

Unfortunately, it is 1923 New York, not Elizabethan England. And Jay insists that the public has no desire to see Mr. Bert Savoy in *Twelfth Night.* He says they only want to see me as a jester talking about the exploits of Margie.

AGNES

Nonsense!

BERT

I have become overshadowed by my own creation.

AGNES

Margie is a brilliant creation, but nothing compared to you.

BERT smiles, then changes the subject:

BERT

Would you help me, Agnes? I have been having trouble with this last section.

AGNES

Yes, of course.

BERT

What will become of this? As I am man,
My state is desperate . . .

As I am man,
My state is desperate . . .

AGNES

. . . for my master's love

BERT

Yes.

As I am man,
My state is desperate . . . for my master's love.
As . . .

AGNES

As I am woman . . .

BERT

As I am woman, now alas the day!
What . . .

AGNES

What thriftless sighs shall poor Olivia breathe!

BERT

It's useless. I cannot seem to remember these lines!

AGNES

What will become of this? As I am man,
My state is desperate for my master's love;
As I am woman, now alas the day!
What thriftless sighs shall poor Olivia breathe!
O time! thou must untangle this, not I;
It is too hard a knot for me to untie!

BERT

Why Agnes! Your talents are limitless!

AGNES

I walked the boards myself once. But now I have taken a different role.

BERT

Do you regret it?

AGNES

Oh no! I am quite content. We must make the most of what we have at every moment. I do not look back.

BERT

You are a bundle of surprises, Agnes.

AGNES

As are you, Mr. Savoy.

BERT

Thank you.

AGNES

For what?

BERT

Never mind. I believe it is time we got out of here. I shall see you tomorrow, my love.

BERT and AGNES exit.

Lights up to reveal JAY in the dressing room. It is the next day.

BERT enters.

JAY

Where have you been. You are late!

BERT

I do not have to answer to you, Jay. I am my own person.

JAY

Stevens will be here any moment. We don't have time to get into another argument. Before he gets here, we need to plan what we will discuss with him.

BERT

Don't you trust me, Jay?

JAY

No, Bertie, that is the point. We must use this second interview to keep our names in the papers. We need to get some good jokes in there to entice the public to see the show.

BERT

And may I not throw in a few mentions of something with a bit more substance?

JAY

Such as?

BERT

Such as our plans to break into motion pictures.

JAY

We have no plans to break into motion pictures.

BERT

Yes, but, if we can get it printed in the papers, perhaps a producer will approach us and. . . .

JAY

Stick to the jokes, Bertie. It's your forte. I will handle the publicity.

BERT

Just like you handled the story about me punching my wife?

JAY

I know the image that we need to portray. It worked, didn't it?

BERT

Worked my nerves, yes. That is not what I want people to know about me. I would much rather they hear of my plans to perform Shakespeare.

JAY

Not this again. Bert, the public does not want to see you perform Shakespeare. You are more of a Fanny Brice, not a Charlotte Cushman.

BERT

I love my Fanny—but the world has need of only one of her. She is a singular talent.

JAY

People want to see you in a gown delivering jokes about Margie.

BERT

Cushman played the men's roles in Shakespeare. So she left the women's roles to me. . . .

JAY

Must you win every argument?

BERT

I am a master of reinventing myself, dearie, and it is time the public saw a new side of me.

JAY

Why change when you are on the top of the world?

BERT

This is the top? How utterly depressing.

JAY

Last year, when we were on tour, you were thrilled with your life and our success.

BERT

It has become tiresome, Jay. *You* have become tiresome.

JAY

What is it you want?

BERT

I want to continue to make them laugh. But I am capable of doing that with Shakespeare's lines, not Margie's.

JAY

Can we end this? This is not the time for this inane discussion.

BERT

You just have to be the boss, don't you?

JAY

When Stevens gets here, follow my lead. Please, Bertie.

BERT

You want me to simply repeat some tired old jokes? Should the public not hear something more refreshing about us?

JAY

To satisfy you, toward the end of the interview, I will bring the conversation 'round to some of our upcoming benefits. Is that refreshing enough?

BERT

I am happy to do some charity benefit for the Field Artillery now and again, but that is not what people want to hear about.

JAY

Please, stop quarreling with me. He will be here any minute. Just do what you do best. I will feed you the setups, and you follow through with the jokes. Can you do that, please?

BERT

I know how to perform, Jay. Stop patronizing.

JAY

And I want us to get in the new line we've been working on. Let me handle the introduction, and I will steer the conversation to . . .

BERT

Jay, stop. I know what to do.

AGNES knocks and sticks her head in.

AGNES

Mr. Stevens to see you, boys.

JAY

Thank you, Agnes. Send him in.

AGNES

And stop bickering! I can hear you two clear down the hall!

BERT

Yes, mother.

AGNES

You're like an old married couple.

BERT

That we are, Agnes, that we are.

JAY

Don't be ridiculous. Agnes, please. . . .

AGNES

Yes, sir.

AGNES leaves to get STEVENS.

JAY

(To BERT:) Please, go behind the screen, and get yourself ready to make an entrance. I'll handle the introductions.

BERT

(Mocking:) Yes sir! Right away, sir!

BERT goes behind screen as AGNES ushers STEVENS in.

AGNES

(Announcing:) Mr. Stevens.

JAY

Aaah Stevens! How nice it is to see you again. Thank you for coming back to feature us in a new article.

STEVENS

My readers can't get enough of the two of you. Where is Mr. Savoy?

BERT

(From behind the dressing screen:) Forgive me, Stevens, I will be right out. I am absolutely frazzled today. Stayed out too late last night. Mr. Garrity threw the most marvelous party. You should have been with us!

JAY

That's Bert's new line for next year—"You should have been with us." How do you like it?

STEVENS

It's good. I'd have to hear in context of your act, of course.

JAY

Perhaps it will become immortal along with "You must come over" and "You don't know the half of it, dearie"? What do you think?

BERT

(Coming around from the screen:) You should have been with us. Yes, you should have been with us! You should have been . . .

JAY

That's enough of that, Bertie.

BERT

I'm glad you came to interview us, Mr. Stevens. Tell us what to say, and we'll say it! Haha!

STEVENS

Yes, now. . . .

BERT

I must change the subject long enough to see if Mr. Brennan has formally introduced you to our Mrs. Jones here.

JAY

Oh, yes, how rude of me. Mr. Stevens, Mrs. Jones.

AGNES

How do, Mr. Stevens.

STEVENS

(Shaking her hand) Hello, Mrs. Jones.

BERT

Are you surprised that I don't prefer a male dresser? No offense, Mrs. Jones.

AGNES

None taken.

STEVENS

Why, yes. Why do you employ a female for the job?

BERT

I always feel safer in a woman's hands. Julian Eltinge had an old man for years, but when he heard *I* had a woman, he tried it—and now he says he wouldn't have any other sex in his dressing room. He takes his cues from me, you know.

JAY

Bertie, I'm sure Mr. Stevens does not want to hear about Eltinge. He came to see you.

BERT

Besides, you cannot depend on a male dresser in a show like this, with so many girls in it. Just when you want him to lace you up, he is out in the wings with the women.

AGNES

Oh, Mr. Savoy, you are wicked!

BERT

Why put temptation in the poor devil's way? Anyhow, Steve, I would not trade Agnes for ten men!

STEVENS

You relate more to women, then? Is that the angle?

STEVENS jots notes as the interview continues.

BERT

Believe me, it's the *women* who've made me who I am.

JAY

Um, yes. . . . Like the chorus girls! Wasn't one of the girls just telling you about the time she was out to dinner with a man? Remember? The lights were dim and the music soft and the wine cold, and her date said, "I've never been in a place like this before." And she said . . .

BERT

"I'm out with an amateur!"

STEVENS

(To AGNES:) Are these two always like this?

AGNES

Every night!

JAY

And what about the joke you told onstage tonight?

STEVENS

What was it?

BERT

Yes, what was it?

JAY

About the girl and her friend who had just seen Douglas Fairbanks in *The Three Musketeers* at the picture house? They passed a bookstore window, and it was full of the Dumas romance. . . .

BERT

"Ain't the printing press wonderful?" said the other girl—"they've got the book out already!"

JAY

You should have heard the audience laugh! They screamed.

BERT

Enough of this small talk. I'm sure Mr. Stevens is tired of all these antics.

JAY

No, no. Our little stories are just what you need for your article. Isn't that right, Mr. Stevens?

STEVENS

Well, yes, but . . .

BERT

Perhaps we can steer this conversation in a new direction?

JAY

Steer? No! You don't have a driver's license, Bertie!

BERT

I'm putting the brakes on, dearie. Follow *my* lead for once, won't you?

JAY

Ha ha. Bert, you've just given me the most wonderful inspiration for a new joke. May I see you outside? Excuse us, Mr. Stevens. We must strike while the iron's hot! We'll just be a minute.

JAY rushes BERT out of the dressing room.

STEVENS

Is that part of the act?

AGNES

Oh yes! Always joking, those two. They're wonderful, aren't they? They're more modest than the girls. They're just like my own boys.

JAY and BERT can be heard arguing with one another in the hall. AGNES tries to distract STEVENS so he will not hear them.

And when one of 'em gets to grumbling to the other, I say, "Maybe he's nervous tonight, so don't pay any attention," and smooth it over.

STEVENS

They're quite a pair.

AGNES

Two halves of a whole.

JAY and BERT reenter. BERT takes a seat at the dressing table and begrudgingly continues with the jokes that JAY insists he share.

JAY

Now, where were we? Oh, yes! Bert, tell Mr. Stevens about the time you made Edison laugh.

STEPHENS

Edison?

JAY

Yes, the great inventor! And, later, back at the theater, *(urging BERT to complete the joke:)* you told one of the girls . . .

BERT

I told one of the girls, "I don't give a damn—"

AGNES

Oh my!

BERT

The very word I used!—"I don't give a damn if the audience laughs tonight, because I just made the great Thomas Edison laugh!" And the girl says to me, "Did you know that Edison's deaf?"

AGNES laughs.

Well, enough of that. Agnes, be a dear, and help me with this wig.

AGNES begins to help BERT at the dressing table take off his wig.

STEVENS

Tell me, do you think female impersonators ought to get married?

BERT

(A pause.) Yes, Mr. Stevens, I do. Why do you ask?

STEVENS

We've all heard the rumors about you and your wife, Mr. Savoy.

BERT

Former wife. But let's not talk about marriage. Let's talk motion pictures!

JAY

No!

BERT

Yes! We are going into movies, did you know, Mr. Stevens?

STEVENS

You are going into the movies?

BERT

My dear, I'm so glad you asked me, I'm so glad! We would have gone long ago, only one hates to go to Siberia, doesn't one?

JAY

Siberia?

STEVENS

Why Siberia?

BERT

I mean Los Angeles. I always get those two foreign countries mixed up like that!

STEVENS

And will you prefer making movies to working on the stage here in New York?

BERT

I'm mad—I'm mad about the movies!

STEVENS

Are you going to wear those clothes?

BERT

Yes, Jay and I are going just as we are, my dear, and throw ourselves at the mercy of the public. Five reel comedies. Can you see us doing five reels? I ask you, my dear!

STEVENS

When do you start? And who is the producer?

JAY

Those are secrets which we cannot reveal yet.

BERT

(Annoyed) Mr. Stevens, do you know what just popped into my head? That old line: "As I am man, / My state is desperate . . ."

STEVENS

What's that from?

BERT

Twelfth Night. Have you not heard about our Shakespeare plans?

STEVENS

Why, no.

JAY

We don't have the time to get into that now.

BERT

(Ignoring JAY) Yes! Next season, I will appear in a series of Shakespearean matinees. I believe I will start with Viola in *Twelfth Night.*

Pause.

STEVENS

And. . . .

BERT

And what?

STEVENS

Is this a setup for a joke?

BERT

No joke, Stevens. If we are seriously received, it might be the dawn of a new career. For both of us.

STEVENS

I can't determine whether or not I am being spoofed. *(To AGNES:)* Can you?

BERT

It is true, Stevie. I can joke of Margie's exploits one minute, and deliver Shakespeare's lines the next. We are all capable of being whomever we choose. People are protean. We are chameleons. How about you, Mr. Stevens? Would you not enjoy being someone else for a change?

STEVENS

Oh, heavens, no. Me playing multiple parts? No—I couldn't imagine such a thing!

JAY

Never you mind this Shakespeare business. Or chameleons. Or whatever it is we are talking about now. Have you heard about our latest benefit? Bert will be challenging Julian Eltinge in the boxing ring at the end of this season.

BERT

WHAT?!

STEVENS

Boxing?! Really?

JAY

Yes. It's all for charity, of course.

STEVENS

Mr. Savoy! You—a pugilist?!

BERT

I can hardly believe it myself.

STEVENS

Well, there was that incident with your wife!

BERT

Former wife. And the truth behind that is . . .

JAY

Bert will box Eltinge anywhere in the vicinity of New York for charity. We will forfeit a thousand dollars in good faith.

BERT

A thousand. . . . ! I thought we weren't going to talk about Eltinge?

JAY

There's no animus in the challenge, of course, but we thought we could draw a good house for a charitable project before our next season begins. Can you picture it? The two greatest female illusionists of our time boxing. . . .

BERT

I am not an illusionist.

JAY

They'll put up quite a good fight, I assure you!

STEVENS

This boxing scoop is a gem! Thank you!

JAY

Mr. Stevens, do you have enough for your feature? Are there any last questions we can answer for you?

STEVENS

Let me consult my notes here. . . . Ah, yes: I am interested in how you two met. Can you tell me something about your past?

BERT

Can't. It's closed for repairs.

STEVENS

That's a good line.

BERT

My word, let the past lie. If you don't, we will. We are what we are today. Isn't that right, Agnes?

JAY

What difference does it make how anybody started? Anything else you'd like to . . .

BERT

But if you insist. Let me tell you about how we met. My, but he was Ritz! He had borrowed a bulldog. . . .

STEVENS

A bulldog?

BERT

Yes! And he brought it to the theater on a leash. . . .

JAY

Bert, old boy, let us stay in the present, shall we?

BERT

Yes, Jay. Old boy. Mr. Stevens, you must come over. We have an apartment on Forty-fifth Street. You must come over. We insist—don't we Jay?—on having your initials carved on our piano. Everyone's played on it but the Pope. You must come over.

STEVENS

You are exactly the same offstage as on. You make up your stuff as you go along, don't you?!

JAY

Does she ever. I never know what she's going to say next.

BERT

Yes.

JAY

She breaks me up. Every night.

AGNES senses the tension between JAY and BERT, tries to ease the situation.

AGNES

Perhaps it's not my place, but, Mr. Stevens, these two really must be getting ready. . . .

STEVENS

Oh, yes, I understand. Thank you for this opportunity to speak with you again. I think I have some real gold here to share with my readers.

BERT

Bye now.

JAY

Yes, goodbye. And thank you!

STEVENS exits.

And thank *you*, Agnes. I thought we'd never get him out of here.

BERT

You want me to fight Eltinge? Eltinge? That . . .

BERT and JAY

. . . fat cow. . . .

JAY

I thought readers would . . .

BERT

I am not going to have you create opprobrious circumstances in my personal life just to . . .

JAY

Please, please, stop!

BERT

And how dare you belittle my ideas about appearing in Shakespeare! You don't believe I have the talent, do you?

JAY

I am more than certain you can be whoever you want to be, Bertie. *(Mocking:)* "We are chameleons." But it's not about what you want. We must think about what the public wants.

BERT

Haley doesn't think Shakespeare is so far-fetched. I was discussing it with him yesterday. . . .

JAY

Then get Haley to produce you. You don't need me, do you?

BERT

Perhaps not. Besides, I think Haley would make a fine producer. He has some solid ideas about how . . .

JAY

Haley's a child, Bert.

BERT

And you, the adult, are so much better? You must stop trying to make a man out of me just to sell some newspapers and some tickets.

JAY

You *are* a man, Bertie.

BERT

That is enough! I am exhausted by you.

JAY

And that is precisely why my doctor advised me to move out of our home, Bertie. You are not the only one who is exhausted by all this. And, speaking of our home. . . .

BERT

My home.

JAY

Why on earth are you inviting Stevens to play our piano? We cannot have . . .

BERT

I can have whomever I wish over to *my* home, Jay, to play *my* piano. And it's Haley's home now, too. You do realize that he has moved in with me?

JAY

Yes, I suspected as much.

BERT

Are you jealous? Green is not . . .

JAY

Will you end it?

BERT

End what? My life?

JAY

No, of course not. That is not what I meant.

BERT

You would love it if I were no longer here. Then you would collect from my insurance policy.

JAY

Please let's stop talking about dying. You are not going to die.

BERT

One day I will, Jay. And then what will you do?

JAY

I cannot think that far into the future. For now, I am going to take a trip to French Lick Springs. On my doctor's advice.

BERT

That doctor needs to mind his own business. Well, you go on ahead to your French Lick Springs—what a positively stupid name. I am going to get away, too. Haley has invited Ohio and I to the beach and . . .

JAY

Haley, Haley, Haley. Please enough with Haley!

BERT

Jealous?

JAY

(Exasperated) Aaaaaah!

BERT

Agnes, help me get dressed. This man is a cretin. Jay, get out.

JAY

Bertie. . . .

BERT

NOW!

BERT exits. AGNES helps BERT as he finishes getting out of his costume.

AGNES

Mr. Savoy, I . . .

BERT

Please, Agnes. For once, let's not talk, shall we?

AGNES

Yes, ma'am.

Thunder is heard.

STEVENS enters, speaks directly to the audience.

STEVENS

I never published that interview. The next article I wrote about Savoy went something like this:

June 29, 1923. "Thespians Mourn for Actor Killed by Bolt of Lightning. More than 1,500 persons attended the services today at the Funeral Church for Bert Savoy, the comedian who was killed Tuesday at Long Beach by a bolt of lightning."

AGNES has left. We see BERT alone as STEVENS continues with the obituary:

"It was the first time Broadway has been affected by death. When the news came it was as though the same electric bolt that killed Savoy had stunned the street. The chapel was banked with flowers, one beautiful wreath marked, 'Husband' being the gift of Mrs. Anna Savoy, the actor's divorced wife. The Flame-Dancer, Klondike Kate, sent a huge bunch of roses with the inscription, 'The world will miss your laughter.' And a bunch of orchids was accompanied by a card which read only 'From Margie.'"

"Jay Brennan, Savoy's partner for many years was so deeply affected that he had to be led from the chapel."

AGNES leads JAY in. He sits in a chair. Solemn.

AGNES continues reading STEVENS' obituary in a newspaper she is carrying:

AGNES

"Jay Brennan, Savoy's partner for many years was so deeply affected that he had to be led from the chapel. Savoy and Brennan's production contract called for $1,250 weekly. They recently reappeared in vaudeville at $1,500."

JAY

Vulgar how easily they print this stuff. I do not want people to know our salaries.

STEVENS

It is not about what you want. This is what the public wants.

STEVENS exits. AGNES continues reading:

AGNES

"There was a strong attachment between him and Mr. Brennan. Several months before the tragedy each took out a $50,000 insurance policy in favor of the other. They had a contract binding them for life. Once when interviewed for a New York paper, Brennan said: 'Don't mention me' . . ."

JAY

That is true.

AGNES

(Reading:) ". . . while Mr. Savoy privately told the reporter: 'Whatever you write, give Jay the best of it.'"

JAY

Oh! *(Cries.)*

AGNES

(Reading:) "Mr. Brennan's hair, once sleek black, is now tinged with white. He has aged many years seemingly overnight. It is difficult to think of harlequins of such an audacious mold being touched by grief."

"A funeral cortege of thirty automobiles drove to Woodlawn Cemetery."

Lights out on BERT, who exits.

AGNES

Those orchids, they were so lovely. Who do you suppose . . .

JAY

Don't, Agnes. Please let's not talk, shall we?

AGNES

Yes.

They remain quiet for a moment. HALEY enters. AGNES sees him first.

AGNES

Mr. Haley.

HALEY

Agnes. Would you give us a moment?

AGNES

Yes, of course. *(To JAY:)* Do you need anything?

JAY

No, I am fine.

AGNES exits.

What do you want, Haley?

HALEY

I don't want to upset you.

JAY

You're not. I saw you at the funeral. You have every right to mourn with the rest of us.

HALEY

Thank you.

JAY

He tried to make me jealous of you these past months.

HALEY

It was you he loved. You know that, don't you?

JAY

Yes, I suppose.

HALEY

That's not why I'm here, though.

JAY

What is it?

HALEY

I came to tell you that a woman showed up at the apartment yesterday.

JAY

What woman?

HALEY

Bert's mother.

JAY

He doesn't have a mother. He was an orphan.

HALEY

That's what he told you, but she insists.

JAY

What does she want?

HALEY

She heard of the insurance policy. She wants in.

JAY

Word gets out fast, doesn't it? She's a charlatan. An opportunist. Nothing to be concerned about.

HALEY

I tried to evade her but she overheard me tell someone that I was going to find you today. She has been following me. . . .

IDA MAY enters.

IDA MAY

Mr. Haley, there you are. Is this Mr. Brennan?

HALEY

No. This is . . . a friend.

JAY

James. Call me James.

IDA MAY

James. I am looking for a Mr. Jay Brennan.

HALEY

We have not seen him, but perhaps we can help. What is it you need, Mrs., uh . . . Savoy?

JAY

Or perhaps it is Mrs. McKenzie?

IDA MAY

McKenzie? Heavens no. It is Walker. Ida May Walker.

JAY

Walker?! I see. You understand our surprise, Mrs. Walker. Bert had told us that he had no mother.

IDA MAY

Oh my, no! Why would he say that? We were very close. Very close. In fact, he visited me in Chicago just last year.

JAY

I was in Chicago with him last year. I do not recall him talking about his mother.

IDA MAY

Oh, yes. He told me that I was named sole beneficiary in his will. In fact, he wanted me to resign my position in Chicago and come to New York to keep up his home!

HALEY

He did?!

IDA MAY

Oh, yes. He has a fine apartment on Forty-fourth Street. I have been there many a time.

HALEY

Forty-*fourth* Street?

IDA MAY

Yes! And he has a piano and everything! Everyone's played on it but the Pope, he says!

JAY

What?

IDA MAY

The Pope. Please, gentlemen, where can I find Mr. Brennan?

HALEY

I am sorry, Mrs. Walker. You seem to be under the impression that we knew Mr. Savoy better than we did.

JAY

It appears that we knew him hardly at all.

HALEY

Unfortunately, we are not aware of the things you've told us.

JAY

And we have no idea how you might find Mr. Brennan. Good luck to you.

IDA MAY

Yes, well. . . . I have a claim here, so I guess I will consult a lawyer, I will!

JAY

You do that now.

IDA MAY

And don't think I want this money for myself. Oh no! I am going to use it to pay for a proper tombstone for my dear boy. *(She produces a handkerchief and appears to dab a tear from her eye.)* Yes! It will read, "He made the world laugh / Erected by his mother." The Walker family wants the world to know how proud we were of him!

HALEY

Yes, that is admirable, isn't it, James?

JAY

Oh my, yes. Well. . . . Good day to you.

IDA MAY

G'day.

IDA MAY exits.

HALEY

Thoughts?

JAY

She is a crackpot, for sure. But that only makes me think she may very well be his mother. Who can say?

HALEY

She knew that line about the Pope. He used that line all the time.

JAY

I don't know, Haley, I don't know. Even in death, the man is exhausting.

They sit silently together for a moment.

HALEY

What will you do now?

JAY

I would like to come back to the apartment.

HALEY

The one on Forty-*fourth* Street?

JAY

Ha! Yes. If you will allow it.

HALEY

Of course. That apartment was just as much yours as his. But that's not what I meant. What will you do now with your act?

JAY

Don't tell me *you* want in on the act?

HALEY

(Laughing) No!

JAY

I can't go it alone. I am the feeder, not the headliner. I suppose I will hire an actor to take over Bert's part.

HALEY

No one can replace him.

JAY

I am well aware of that. Perhaps I will find a real woman to take on the role. . . .

HALEY

A real woman?

JAY

I am not sure I know what that is anymore. Oh, Haley, I cannot think about this right now. "O time! thou must untangle this, not I; / It is too hard a knot for me to untie!"

HALEY

What?

JAY

Shakespeare.

HALEY

Sorry. I never could understand Shakespeare.

JAY

Bert told me you wanted to produce him in *Twelfth Night* next season.

HALEY

We never talked about that. Me? Producing Shakespeare? Can you imagine?!

JAY laughs, realizing it had been another of BERT's lies.

What is it?

JAY

Nothing, Haley.

HALEY

Shall we go?

JAY

Tell me one thing.

HALEY

Yes?

JAY

What really happened on that beach? Was he really yelling up to the sky: Mercy! Miss God! and all that?

HALEY

Oh no. It was awful, Mr. Brennan.

JAY

Please call me, Jay.

HALEY

Yes. Jay. You don't want to know.

JAY

Tell me.

HALEY

He was in the water. Alone. He had been melancholy the entire afternoon.

BERT enters in his bathing costume, wading in the imaginary water. This time, the story is played truthfully, not as a routine.

The sky turned black in an instant. It all happened so fast.

BERT

Haley? Ohio? Where are you? I hate storms. Always have! . . . I'm not joking. . . . Don't leave me here by myself. I don't want to be alone!

HALEY

He ran wildly for a few moments, found Ohio just as. . . .

Huge thunderclap is heard. When the lights come back up, BERT is gone.

JAY

That'll be quite enough out of you, Miss God.

HALEY

That *is* a good line.

JAY

You don't know the half of it, dearie.

HALEY

Ha!

JAY

She was correct about one thing.

HALEY

Who?

JAY

The mother. The supposed mother.

HALEY

What?

JAY

He made the world laugh. Hell, he made *me* laugh. And that is not an easy thing to do. Oh, Haley, what am I going to do without him?

HALEY

I can't say. But don't sit here by yourself. Why don't you join me? "You must come over."

JAY

Very good.

HALEY

I learned from the best. "You should have been with us."

JAY

I should have been.

JAY smiles, takes HALEY's arm and puts his head on his shoulder. They exit together.

Blackout.